# INTRODUCTION



BY

SIR JOHN WOODROFFE

Fourth Edition

Martino Publishing
Mansfield Centre, CT
2012

*Martino Publishing*
*P.O. Box 373,*
*Mansfield Centre, CT 06250 USA*

www.martinopublishing.com

ISBN 978-1-61427-339-4



Cover design by T. Matarazzo

*Printed in the United States of America On 100% Acid-Free Paper*

# INTRODUCTION TO TANTRA ŚĀSTRA

BY

SIR JOHN WOODROFFE

Fourth Edition

PUBLISHERS :

GANESH & CO. (MADRAS) PRIVATE LTD.

1963

1st Edition 1913
2nd Edition 1952
3rd Edition 1956
4th Edition 1963

G. S. Press, Madras.

CONTENTS

| | | |
|---|---|---|
| Mount Kailāsa | .. | 1 |
| Śiva and Śaktī | .. | 4 |
| Guṇa | .. | 18 |
| The Worlds (Lokas) | .. | 24 |
| Inhabitants of the Worlds | .. | 26 |
| Varṇa | .. | 31 |
| Aśrama | .. | 32 |
| Macrocosm and Microcosm | .. | 34 |
| The Ages | .. | 36 |
| The Scriptures of the Ages | .. | 40 |
| The Human Body | .. | 42 |
| The Three Temperaments | .. | 58 |
| Guru and Śiṣya | .. | 65 |
| Initiation : Dīkṣā | .. | 68 |
| Abhiṣeka | .. | 70 |
| Sādhana | .. | 72 |
| Worship | .. | 74 |
| Yoga | .. | 123 |
| Sin and Virtue—Karma | .. | 140 |
| Four Aims of Being (Dharma, Artha, Kāma, Mokṣa) | .. | 145 |
| Siddhi | .. | 152 |

This book is the "Introduction" to The Great Liberation (Mahānirvāṇa Tantra), frequently referred to in Sir John Woodroffe's "Principles of Tantra" and his other works. . . . A key to the fuller understanding of all Tantrik literature.

ŚRI YANTRA

# MOUNT KAILĀSA

THE scene of the revelation of Mahānirvāṇa-Tantra is laid in Himālaya, the " Abode of Snow, " a holy land weighted with the traditions of the Āryan race. Here in these lofty uplands, encircled with everlasting snows, rose the great mountain of the north, the Sapta-Kula-Parvata. Hence the race itself came, and there its early legends have their setting. There are still shown at Bhimudiyar the caves where the sons of Pāṇḍu and Draupadi rested, as did Rāma and his faithful wife at the point where the Kosi joins the Sītā in the grove of Aśoka trees. In these mountains Munis and Ṛṣis lived. Here also is the Kṣetra of Śiva Mahādeva, where his spouse Pārvatī, the daughter of the Mountain King, was born, and where Mother Ganges also has her source. From time immemorial pilgrims have toiled through these mountains to visit the three great shrines at Gangotri,[1] Kedarnath,[2] and Badrinath.[3] At Kangri, further north, the pilgrims make the parikrama of Mount Kailāsa (Kang Rinpoche), where Śiva is said to dwell. This nobly towering

---

1. Source of the Ganges.

2. A maṭha and temple dedicated to Śri Sadāśiva in charge of the Saiva ascetics called Jaṅgama. The Devatā is also worshipped at four other places along the Himalayan chain—Tungnath, Rudranath, Madhmaheśwar, and Kalpeśvar. These and the first-named form the "Panchkedar."

3. A celebrated temple dedicated to an incarnation of the Deva Viṣṇu, who from Kūrmācala is said to have descended in his Kūrma form. As to Badarika see Mahābhārata c. 92 Āraṇya-parvan.

peak rises to the north-west of the sacred Manasarowar Lake (Mapham Yum-tso) from amidst the purple ranges of the lower Kangri Mountains. The paradise of Śiva is a summerland of both lasting sunshine and cool shade, musical with the song of birds and bright with undying flowers. The air, scented with the sweet fragrance of Mandāra chaplets, resounds with the music and song of celestial singers and players. The Mount is Gaṇa-parvata, thronged with trains of Spirits (devayoni), of which the opening chapter of Mahānirvāṇa-Tantra speaks.

And in the regions beyond rises Mount Meru, centre of the world-lotus. Its heights, peopled with spirits, are hung with clusters of stars as with wreaths of Mālatī flowers. In short, it is written :[1] "He who thinks of Himācala, though he should not behold him, is greater than he who performs all worship in Kāśi (Benares). In a hundred ages of the Devas I could not tell thee of the glories of Himācala. As the dew is dried up by the morning sun, so are the sins of mankind by the sight of Himācala."

It is not, however, necessary to go to the Himālayan Kailāśa to find Śiva. He dwells wheresoever his worshippers, versed in Kula-tattva, abide,[2] and His mystic mount is to be sought in the thousand-petalled lotus[3] (sahasrāra-padma) in the body of every human jīva, hence called Śiva-sthāna, to which all, wheresoever situate, may repair when they have learned how to achieve the way thither.

Śiva promulgates His teaching in the world below in the works known as Yāmala, Dāmara, Śiva-Sūtra,[4] and in the Tantras which exist in the form of dialogues between

1. Skanda-Purāṇa.

2. Kulārṇava-Tantra (chap. ix).

3. See Tripurāsāra, cited in Bhāskararāya's Commentary on Lalitā-sahasranāma, verse 17. Guroh sthānam hi Kailasaṁ as the Yoginī-Tantra (chap. i) says.

4. Of which the Śiva-Sūtra-Vimarśini is a Commentary.

the Devatā and his Śakti, the Devī in Her form as Pārvatī. According to the Gāyatri-Tantra,[1] the Deva Gaṇeśa first preached the Tantra to the Devayoni on Mount Kailāsa, after he had himself received them from the mouth of Śiva.

After a description of the mountain, the dialogue opens with a question from Pārvatī[2] in answer to which and those which succeed it, Śiva unfolds His doctrine on the subjects with which Mahā-nirvāṇa-Tantra deals.

---

1. Chapter X.

2. As the Devī is here the sishya, this Tantra is in the form called Agama

# ŚIVA AND ŚAKTI

THAT eternal immutable existence which transcends the turīya and all other states in the unconditioned Absolute, the supreme Brahman or Para-brahman, without Prakṛti (niṣkala) or Her attributes (nir-guṇa), which, as being the inner self and knowing subject, can never be the object of cognition, and is to be apprehended only through yoga by the realization of the Self (ātma-jnāna), which It is. For as it is said, " Spirit can alone know Spirit. " Being beyond mind, speech, and without name, the Brahman was called "Tat," "That," and then "Tat Sat," "That which is." For the sun, moon, and stars, and all visible things, what are they but a glimpse of light caught from "That" (Tat)?

Brahman is both niṣkala and sakala. Kalā is Prakṛti. The niṣkala-Brahman or Para - brahman is the Tat when thought of as without Prakṛti (Prakṛteranyā). It is called sakala when with Prakṛti.[1] As the substance of Prakṛti is the three guṇas It is then sa-guṇa, as in the previous state It was nir-guṇa. Though in the latter state It is thought of as without Śakti, yet (making accommodation to human speech) in It potentially exists Śakti, Its power and the whole universe produced by It. To say, however, that the Śakti exists in the Brahman is but a form of speech, since It and Śakti are, in fact, one, and Śakti is eternal (Anādi-rūpā).[2] She is Brahma-rūpā and

---

1. Śāradā-tilaka (chap. i), and chap. i of Śāktānanda-taraṅgiṇi ("Waves of Bliss for Śaktas"), both Tantrika works of great authority.

2. Praṇamya prakṛtiṁ nityaṁ paramātma-svarūpiṇiṁ (loc. cit. Śaktānanda-taraṅgiṇi).

both viguṇa (nir-guṇa) and sa-guṇā; the Caitanyarūpiṇī-Devī, who manifests all bhūta. She is the Ānandarūpiṇī-Devī, by whom the Brahman manifests Itself,[1] and who, to use the words of the Śārada, pervades the universe as does oil the sesamum seed.

In the beginning the Niṣkala-Brahman alone existed. In the beginning there was the One. It willed and became many. Ahaṁ-bahu-syāṁ — " may I be many. " In such manifestation of Śakti the Brahman is known as the lower (apara) or manifested Brahman, who, as, the subject of worship, is meditated upon with attributes. And, in fact, to the mind and sense of the embodied spirit (jīva) the Brahman has body and form. It is embodied in the forms of all Devas and Devīs, and in the worshipper himself. Its form is that of the universe, and of all things and beings therein.

As Śruti says : " He saw " (Sa aikṣata, ahaṁ bahu syām prajāyeya). He thought to Himself " May I be many. " "Sa aikṣhata " was itself a manifestation of Śakti, the Paramāpūrva-nirvāṇa-śakti, or Brahman as Śakti.[2] From the Brahman, with Śakti (Paraśakti-maya) issued Nāda (Śiva-Śakti as the " Word " or " Sound "), and from Nāda, Bindu appeared. Kālicharana[3] in his commentary on the Ṣatcakra-nirūpaṇa says that Śiva and Nirvāṇa - Śakti bound by a mayik bond and covering, should be thought of as existing in the form of Paraṁ Bindu.

The Sāradā[4] says : Saccidānanda - vibhavāt sakalāt parameśvarāt āsīcchaktistato nādo, nādād bindu-samud-bhavah. ("From Parameśvara vested with the wealth of

---

1. Kubjika-Tantra, 1st Patala.
2. Ṣat-cakra-nirupaṇa. Commentary on verse 49, "Serpent Power".
3. Ibid., verse 37.
4. Śāradā-tilaka (chap i).

Saccidānanda and with Prakṛti (sakala) issued Śakti; from Śakti came Nāda and from Nāda was born Bindu"). The state of subtle body which is known as Kāma-kalā is the mūla of mantra. The term mūla-mantrātmikā, when applied to the Devī, refers to this subtle body of Hers known as the Kāma-kalā.[1] The Tantra also speaks of three Bindus, namely, Śiva-maya, Śakti-maya, and Śiva-Śakti-maya.[2]

The paraṁ-bindu is represented as a circle, the centre of which is the brahma-pada, or place of Brahman, wherein are Prakṛti-Puruṣa, the circumference of which is encircling māyā.[3] It is on the crescent of nirvāṇa-kalā the seventeenth, which is again in that of amā-kala, the sixteenth digit (referred to in the text) of the moon-circle (Candra-maṇḍala), which circle is situate above the Sun-Circle (Sūrya-maṇḍala), the Guru and the haṁsah, which are in the pericarp of the thousand-petalled lotus (sahasrāra-padma). Next to the Bindu is the fiery Bodhinī, or Nibodhikā (v. post). The Bindu, with the Nirvāṇa-kalā, Nibodhikā, and Amā-kalā, are situated in the lightning-like inverted triangle[4] known as "A, Ka, Tha," and which is so called because at its apex is A; at its right base is Ka; and at its left base Tha. It is made up of forty-eight letters (mātṛkā): the sixteen vowels running from A to Ka; sixteen consonants of the kavarga and other groups running from Ka to Tha; and the remaining sixteen from Tha to A.

---

1. See Bhāskararāya's Commentary on the Lalitāsahasranāma, verse 36.

2. Prāṇa-toṣini, (p. 8).

3. Māyābandhanācchaditaprakṛtipuruṣa paraṁ binduh, Commentary to verse 49 of the Ṣat-cakra-nirūpaṇa.

4. The Devī-Purāṇa says that Kuṇḍalini is so called because She has the Śṛṅgātaka or triangle form. the three angles being the iccha, jnana and kriya-Śaktis (see also Yoginī-hridaya).

Inside are the remaining letters (mātṛkā), ha, la (second), and kṣa.[1] As the substance of Devī is mātṛka (mātṛkā-mayī) the triangle represents the "Word" of all that exists. The triangle is itself encircled by the Candra-maṇdala. The Bindu is symbolically described as being like a grain of gram (caṇaka), which under its encircling sheath contains a divided seed. This Paraṁ-bindu is prakṛti-Puruṣa, Śiva-Śakti.[2] It is known as the Śabda-Brahman (the Sound Brahman), or Apara-brahman.[3] A polarization of the two Śiva and Śakti - Tattvas then takes place in Para-śakti-maya. The Devī becomes Unmukhī. Her face turns towards Śiva. There is an unfolding which bursts the encircling shell of Māyā, and creation then takes place by division of Śiva and Śakti or of "Haṁ" and "Sah."[4] The Sāradā says: "The Devatā-paraśakti-maya is again Itself divided, such divisions being known as Bindu, Bīja, and Nāda.[5] Bindu is of the nature of Nāda of Śiva, and Bījā of Śakti, and Nāda has been said to be the relation of these two by those who are versed in all the Āgamas."[6] The Sāradā says that before the bursting of the shell enclosing the Brahma-pada, which, together with its defining circumference, constitutes the Śabda-brahman, an

1. Ṣat-cakra-nirūpaṇa.
2. Ṣat-cakra-nirūpaṇa, Commentary, verse 49.
3. Śāradā-tilaka, (chap. i):

   Bhidyamānat parad bindoravyaktātmaravo'bhavat.
   Sabda-brahmeti taṁ prāhuh.

"From the unfolding Paraṁbindu arose an indistinct sound. This bindu is called the Śabda-brahman."

4. Ṣat-cakra-nirūpaṇa, verse 49.
5. That is, these are three different aspects of It.
6. Chapter I:

   Paraśaktimayâh sākṣāt tridhāsau bhidyate punah.
   Bindurnādo bījam iti tasya bhedāh samīritāh.
   Binduḥ Śivatmako bījaṁ Śaktirnādastayormithah.
   Samavāyah samākhyatāh sarvāga-maviśaradaih.

indistinct sound arose (avyaktātmā-ravo' bhavat). This avyaktanāda is both the first and the last state of Nāda, according as it is viewed from the standpoint of evolution or involution. For Nāda, as Rāghava-bhaṭṭa[1] says, exists in three states. In Nāda are the guṇas (sattva, rajas, and tamas), which form the substance of Prakṛti, which with Śiva It is. When tamo-guṇa predominates Nāda is merely an indistinct or unmanifested (dhvanyatmako'-vyaktanādah[2]) sound in the nature of dhvani. In this state, in which it is a phase of Avyakta-nāda, it is called Nibodhikā, or Bodhinī. It is Nāda when rajo-guṇa is in the ascendant, when there is a sound in which there is something like a connected or combined disposition of the letters.[3] When the sattva-guṇa preponderates Nāda assumes the form of Bindu.[4] The action of rajas on tamas is to veil. Its own independent action effects an arrangement which is only perfected by the emergence of the essentially manifesting sāttvika-guṇa set into play by it. Nāda, Bindu, and Nibodhikā, and the Śakti, of which they are the specific manifestation, are said to be in the form of Sun, Moon, and Fire respectively.[5] Jnāna (spiritual wisdom[6]) is spoken of as fire as it burns up all actions, and the tamo-guṇa is associated with it. For when the effect of cause and effect of action are really known, then action

---

1. See Commentary on verse 48 of the Ṣat-cakra-nirūpaṇa.

2. Tamo-guṇādhikyena kevala-dhvanyātmako'vyakta-nādah. Avyakta is lit. unspoken, hidden, unmanifest, etc.

3. Raja'ādhikyena kiṁcidvarṇa-baddhā-nyāsātmakāh.

4. Sattvādhikyena bindurūpah.

5. Tataśca nāda-bindu-nibodhikāh arkenduvahnirūpāh (Ṣat-cakra, verse 49 note). See also the Śāradā (chap. i), which says te (that is, Raudri, Jyeṣtha, and Vāmā) jñānecchākriyātmano vahnīndvarka-svarūpiṇah.

6. Jnāna is that knowledge which gives liberation. All other knowledge is called vijnāna.

ceases. Ichchhā is the Moon. The moon contains the sixteenth digit, the Amā-kalā with its nectar, which neither increases nor decays, and Ichchhā or will is the eternal precursor of creation. Kriyā is like Sun, for as the Sun by its light makes all things visible, so unless there is action and striving there cannot be realization or manifestation. As the Gītā says: "As one Sun makes manifest all the loka."

The Śabda-Brahman manifests Itself in a triad of energies—knowledge (jnānaśakti), will (icchā-śakti), and action (kriyā-śakti), associated with the three gunas of Prakṛti, tamas, sattva, and rajas. From the Paraṁ Bindu, who is both bindvātmaka and kalātmā—i.e., Śakti—issued Raudrī, Rudra and his Śakti, whose forms are Fire (vahni), and whose activity is knowledge (jnāna); Vāmā and Viśṇu and his Śakti, whose form is the Sun and whose activity is Kriyā (action): and Jyeṣṭhā and Brahmā and his Śakti, whose form is the Moon, and whose activity is desire. The Vāmakeśvara-Tantra says that Tri-purā is threefold, as Brahmā, Viṣṇu, and Iśa; and as the energies desire, wisdom, and action;[1] the energy of will when Brahman would create; the energy of wisdom when She reminds Him, saying "Let this be thus"; and when, thus knowing, He acts, She becomes the energy of action. The Devī is thus Icchā-śakti-jnāna-śakti-kriyā-śakti svarūpiṇi.[2]

Para-Śiva exists as a septenary under the form, firstly, of Śambhu, who is the associate of time (Kāla-bandhu). From Him issues Sadā-Śiva, Who pervades and manifests all things, and then come Iśāna and the triad, Rudra, Viṣṇu and Brahmā, each with their respective Śaktis

---

1. See Prāna-toṣini (pp. 8, 9). Goraksha Sanghita and Bhuta-shuddhi-Tantra. See also Yoginī-Tantra, Part I, chap. x.

2. Lalita, verse 130 (see Bhāskararāya's Commentary).

(without whom they avail nothing[1]) separately and particularly associated with the guṇas, tamas, sattva and rajas. Of these Devas, the last triad, together with Iśāna and Sadā-śiva, are the five Śivas who are collectively known as the Mahā-preta, whose bīja is "Hsauh." Of the Mahā-preta, it is said that the last four form the support and the fifth the seat, of the bed on which the Devī is united with Parama-śiva, in the room of cintāmani stone;[2] on the jewelled island clad with clumps of kadamba and heavenly trees set in the ocean of Ambrosia.[3]

Śiva is variously addressed in this work as Śambhu, Sadā-śiva, Śaṁkara, Maheśvara, etc., names which indicate particular states, qualities and manifestations of the One in its descent towards the many; for there are many Rudras. Thus Sadā-śiva indicates the predominance of the sattva-guṇa. His names are many, 1,008 being given in the sixty-ninth chapter of the Śiva-Purāṇa and in the seventeenth chapter of the Anuśāsana-Parvan of the Mahābhārata.[4]

Śakti is both māyā, that by which the Brahman creating the universe is able to make Itself appear to be

---

1. And so the Kubjika-Tantra (chap. i) says: "Not Brahma, Viṣṇu, Rudra create, maintain, or destroy; but Brahmi, Vaishnavi, Rudrani. Their husbands are but as dead bodies."

2. The "stone which grants all desires" is described in the Rudrayāmala and Brahmānda-Purāṇa. It is the place of origin of all those Mantras which bestow all desired objects (cintita).

3. See Anandalahari of Saṁkaracharya, (verse 8), and Rudrayāmala. According to the Bahurupastaka and Bhairavayāmala, the bed is Śiva, the pillow Maheśana, the matting Śadaśiva, and the four supports Brahma, Hari, Rudra, and Īśaṅa. Hence Devi is called Pancha-preta-mancādhisāyini (verse 174, Lalitasahasranama).

4. See also the Agni, Padma, Bhaviṣyottara, Varāha, Kūrma, Vāmana Purāṇas, and in particular, the Linga and the Kāsikhanda of the Skanda Purâna.

different from what It really is,[1] and mūla-prakṛti, or the unmanifested (avyakta) state of that which, when manifest, is the universe of name and form. It is the primary so-called "material cause," consisting of the equipoise of the triad of guṇa or "qualities" which are sattva (that which manifests) rajas (that which acts), tamas (that which veils and produces inertia). The three guṇas represent Nature as the revelation of spirit, Nature as the passage of descent from spirit to matter, or of ascent from matter to spirit and Nature as the dense veil of spirit.[2] The Devī is thus guṇa-nidhi[3] (treasure-house of guṇa"). Mūla-prakṛti is the womb into which Brahman casts the seed from which all things are born.[4] The womb thrills to the movement of the essentially active rajo-guṇa. The equilibrium of the triad is destroyed and the guṇa, now in varied combinations, evolve under the illumination of Śiva (cit), the universe which is ruled by Maheśvara and Maheśvarī. The dual principles of Śiva and Śakti, which are in such dual form, the product of the polarity manifested in Parāśakti-maya, pervade the whole universe and are present in man in the Svayambhū-Linga of the mūlādhāra and the Devī Kuṇḍalinī, who, in serpent form, encircles it. The Śabda-Brahman assumes in the body of man the form of the Devī Kuṇḍalinī, and as such is in all prāṇi (breathing creatures) and in the shape of letters appears in prose and verse. Kuṇḍala means coiled.

---

1. The Devī Purāna (chap. xiv), speaking of this power of the Supreme, says: "That which is of various cause and effect; the giver of unthought-of fruit which in this world seems like magic or a dream; that is called māyā";

Vicitra-kāryakāranācintitāphalapradā
Svapnendrajālavalloke maya tena prakirtita.

2. See post sub voc, "Guna".

3. Lalitā-sahasra-nāma, (verse 121). For though the gunas are specifically three they have endless modifications.

4. Bhagavad-gītā, (chap. xiv).

Hence Kuṇḍalinī, whose form is that of a coiled serpent, means that which is coiled. She is the luminous vital energy (jīva-śakti) which manifests as prāṇa, She sleeps in the mūlādhāra and has three and a half coils corresponding in number with the three and a half bindus of which the Kubjikā-Tantra speaks. When after closing the ears the sound of Her hissing is not heard death approaches.

From the first avyakta creation issued the second mahat, with its three guṇas distinctly manifested. Thence sprung the third creation ahaṁkāra (selfhood), which is of threefold form—vaikārika, or pure sāttvika ahaṁkāra; the taijasa, or rājasika ahaṁkāra; and the tāmasika or bhūtādika ahamkāra. The latter is the origin of the subtle essences (tan-mātrā) of the Tattvas, ether, air, fire water, earth, associated with sound, touch, sight, taste, and smell, and with the colours—pure transparency, śyāma, red, white, and yellow. There is some difference in the schools as to that which each of the three forms produces but from such threefold form of Ahamkāra issue the Indriya ("senses"), and the Devas Dik, Vāta, Arka, Pracetas, Vahni, Indra, Upendra, Mitra, and the Ashvins. The vaikārika, taijasa, and bhūtādika are the fourth, fifth, and sixth creations, which are known as prākrita, or appertaining to Prakṛti. The rest, which are products of these, such as the vegetable world with its upward life current, animals with horizontal life current and bhūta, preta and the like, whose life current tends downward, constitute the vaikṛta creation, the two being known as the kaumāra creation.

The Goddess (Devī) is the great Śakti. She is Māyā for of Her the māyā which produces the samsāra is. As Lord of māyā She is Mahamāyā.[1] Devī is a-vidyā (nescience)

1. Mahāmāyā without māyā is nir-gunā; and with māyā Sa-guna; Shāktānanda tarangini, Chap. i.

because She binds and vidyā (knowledge) because She liberates and destroys the samsāra.[1] She is Prakṛti,[2] and as existing before creation is the Ādyā (primordial) Śakti. Devī is the vācaka-śakti, the manifestation of Cit in Prakṛti, and the vāchya-śakti, or Cit itself. The Ātmā should be contemplated as Devī.[3] Śakti or Devī is thus the Brahman revealed in Its mother aspect (Śrī-māta)[4] as Creatrix and Nourisher of the worlds. Kālī says of Herself in Yoginī-Tantra[5]: "Saccidānanda-rūpāhaṁ brahmaivāham sphurat-prabham." So the Devī is described with attributes both of the qualified[6] Brahman and (since that Brahman is but the manifestation of the Absolute) She is also addressed with epithets, which denote the unconditioned Brahman.[7] She is the great Mother (Ambikā) sprung from the sacrificial hearth of the fire of the Grand consciousness (cit); decked with the Sun and Moon; Lalitā, "She who plays"; whose play is world-play; whose eyes playing like fish in the beauteous waters of her Divine face, open and shut with the appearance and disappearance of countless worlds now illuminated by her light, now wrapped in her terrible darkness.[8]

The Devī, as Para-brahman, is beyond all form and guṇa. The forms of the Mother of the Universe are

---

1. Śāktānanda-tarangini, (chap. i).

2. Brahma-vaivarta. Purāṇa (chap. i). Prakritikhanda, Nāradīya-Purāṇa.

3. See chap. ii, of Devī-bhāgavata.

4. Devī is worshipped on account of Her soft heart: (komalāntahkaranam). Śāktānanda-tarangini (chap. iii).

5. Part I, Chapter X.

6. Such as Mukunda an aspect of Vishnu. Lalitā-sahasra-nāmā, verse 838.

7. Ibid., verse 153, and Commentator's note to Chapter II where Devi is addressed as Supreme Light (paraṁ-jyotih), Supreme Abode (paraṁdhāma), Supreme of Supreme (parātparā).

8. See the Lalitā-sahasra-nāmā.

threefold. There is first the Supreme (*para*) form, of which, as the Viṣṇu-yāmala says,[1] "none know." There is next her subtle (sūkṣma) form, which consists of mantra. But as the mind cannot easily settle itself upon that which is formless,[2] She appears as the subject of contemplation in Her third, or gross (sthūla), or physical form, with hands and feet and the like as celebrated in the Devī-stotra of the Purānas and Tantras. Devī, who as Prakrti is the source of Brahmā, Viṣṇu, and Maheśvara,[3] has both male and female forms.[4] But it is in Her female forms that she is chiefly contemplated. For though existing in all things, in a peculiar sense female beings are parts of Her.[5] The Great Mother, who exists in the form of all Tantras and all Yantras,[6] is, as the Lalitā says, the "unsullied treasure-house of beauty"; the Sapphire Devī,[7] whose slender waist,[8] bending beneath

---

1. Mātastvat-param-rūpam tanna jānāti kashchana (see chap. iii of Śāktānanda-tarangini).

2. Amūrtaucit-sthrio na syāt tato mūrttiṁ vicintayet (ibid. chap i, as was explained to Himavat by Devī in the Kūrma Purāṇa).

3. Ibid., and as such is called Tripurā (see Bhāskararāya's Commentary on Lalitā, verse 125).

4. Ibid., chap. iii, which also says that there is no eunuch form of God.

5. So in the Chandi (Mārkandeya-Purāna) it is said:

Vidyah samastastava devī bhedah
Striyah samastāh sakalā jagatsu.

See author's "Hymns to the Goddess". The Tantrika more than all men, recognises the divinity of woman, as was observed centuries past by the Author of the Dabistān. The Linga-Purāna also after describing Arundhati, Anasūyā, and Shachi to be each the manifestation of Devī, concludes: "All things indicated by words in the feminine gender are manifestations of Devī." Similarly the Brahma-vaivarta Purāṇa.

6. Sarva-tantra-rūpā; Sarva-yantrātmikā (see Lalitā, verses 205-6).

7. Padma-purāṇa says: "Vishnu ever worships the Sapphire Devī".

8. Āpivara-stana-tating tanurimadhyām (Bhuvaneshvaristotra). "tanūmadhyā (Lalitā, verse 79) Krisodari (Ādyakālisvarūpa stotra, Mahā-nirvāna-Tantra, seventh Ullāsa).

the burden of the ripe fruit of her breasts,[1] swells into jewelled hips heavy[2] with the promise of infinite maternities.[3]

As the Mahādevī[4] She exists in all forms as Sarasvatī, Lakṣmī, Gāyatrī, Durgā, Tripurā-sundarī, Annapūrṇā, and all the Devīs who are avataras of the Brahman.[5]

Devī, as Satī, Umā, Pārvatī, and Gaūri, is spouse of Śiva. It was as Satī prior to Dakṣa's sacrifice (dakṣa-yajna) that the Devī manifested Herself to Śiva[6] in the ten celebrated forms known as the daśa-mahavidya referred to in the text—Kālī, Bagalā, Chinna-mastā, Bhuvaneśvarī, Mātanginī, Shodaśī, Dhūmāvatī, Tripura-sundarī, Tārā, and Bhairavī. When, at the Dakṣayajna She yielded up her life in shame and sorrow at the treatment accorded by her father to Her Husband, Siva took away the body, and, ever bearing it with Him, remained wholly distraught and spent with grief. To save the world from the forces of evil which arose and

---

1. Pinā-stanādye in Karpūrādistotra, pinonnata-payodharâm in Durgā-dhyāna of Devī Purāna: Vakshoja-kumbhāntari in Annapūrnāstava, āpivara-stana-tatim in Bhuvaneshvāristotra; which weight her limbs, hucha-bhara-namitāngim in Sarasvati-dhyāna; annapradāna-niratāng-stana-bhāra-namrām in Anna-pūrnāstava.

2. So it is said in the tenth sloka of the Karpūrākhyastava—samantâdā pinastana jaghanadhrikyauvanavati. Shaṁkarāchārya, in his Tripurā-sundari-stotra speaks of Her nitamba (nitamba-jita-bhūdharām) as excelling the mountain in greatness.

3. The physical characteristics of the Devī in Her swelling breasts and hips are emblematic of Her great Motherhood for She is Shrīmātā (see as to Her litanies. "Hymns to the Goddess", by A. and E. Avalon).

4. She whose body is, as the Devī Purāna says, immeasurable.

5. Śāktānanda-taranginī (chap. iii).

6. In order to display Her power to Her husband, who had not granted, at her request, His permission that she might attend at Dakṣa's sacrifice. See my edition of the "Tantra—tattva", (Principles of Tantra) and for an account of the daśa-mahāvidyā—their yantra and mantra—the daśa-mahāvidyā-upāsana-rahasya of Prasanna Kumāra Shāstri.

grew with the withdrawal of His Divine control, Viṣṇu with His discus (cakra) cut the dead body of Satī, which Śiva bore, into fifty-one[1] fragments, which fell to earth at the places thereafter known as the fifty-one mahā-pitha-sthāna (referred to in the text), where Devi, with Her Bhairava, is worshipped under various names.

Besides the forms of the Devī in the Brahmāṇḍa, there is Her subtle form called Kuṇḍalinī in the body (piṇḍāṇda). These are but some only of Her endless forms. She is seen as one and as many, as it were, but one moon reflected in countless water.[2] She exists, too, in all animals and inorganic things, the universe with all its beauties is, as the Devī-Purāṇa says but a part of Her. All this diversity of form is but the infinite manifestation of the flowering beauty of the One Supreme Life,[3] a doctrine which is nowhere else taught with greater wealth of illustration than in the Śākta-Śastras, and Tantras. The great Bharga in the bright Sun and all devatās, and indeed, all life and being, are wonderful, and are worshipful but only as Her manifestations. And he who worships them otherwise is, in the words of the great Devī-bhāgavata,[4] "like unto a man who, with the light of a clear lamp in his hands, yet falls into some waterless and terrible well." The highest worship for which the sādhaka is qualified (adhikarī) only after external worship[5] and that internal form

1. The number is variously given as 50, 51, and 52.

2. Brahma-vindu Upanishad, 12.

3. See the Third Chapter of the Śāktānanda-taranginī, where it is said: "The Para-brahman, Devī, Śiva, and all other Deva and Devī are but one, and he who thinks them different from one another goes to Hell.".

4. Hymn to Jagad-ambikā in Chapter XIX.

5. Sūta-sanghītā, i.5.3, which divides such worship into Vedic and Tāntrik (see Bhāskararāya"s Commentary on Lalitā, verse 43).

known as sādhāra,[1] is described as nirādhārā. Therein Pure Intelligence is the Supreme Śakti who is worshipped as the very Self, the Witness freed of the glamour of the manifold Universe. By one's own direct experience of Maheśvarī as the Self She is with reverence made the object of that worship which leads to liberation.[2]

1. In which Devi is worshipped in the form made up of sacred syllables according to the instructions of the Guru.

2. See Introduction to Author's "Hymns to the Goddess."

# GUNA

IT cannot be said that current explanations give a clear understanding of this subject. Yet such is necessary, both as affording one of the chief keys to Indian Philosophy and to the principles which govern Sādhana. The term guṇa is generally translated "quality," a word which is only accepted for default of a better. For it must not be overlooked that the three guṇas (Sattva, rajas, and tamas) which are of Prakṛti constitute Her very substance. This being so, all Nature which issues from Her, the Mahā-kāraṇa-svarūpā, is called tri-guṇātmaka, and is composed of the same guṇa in different states of relation to one another. The functions of sattva, rajas, and tamas are to reveal, to make active, and to suppress respectively. Rajas is the dynamic, as sattva and tamas are static principles. That is to say, sattva and tamas can neither reveal nor suppress without being first rendered active by rajas. These guṇas work by mutual suppression.

The unrevealed Prakṛti (avyakta-prakṛti) or Devī is the state of stable equilibrium of these three guṇas. When this state is disturbed the manifested universe appears, in every object of which one or other of the three guṇas is in the ascendant. Thus in Devas as in those who approach the divya state, sattva predominates, and rajas and tamas are very much reduced. That is, their independent manifestation is reduced. They are in one sense still there, for where rajas is not independently active it is operating on sattva to suppress tamas, which appears or disappears to the extent to which it is, or is not, subject to suppression by the revealing principle. In the ordinary human jīva considered as a class, tamas is less reduced than in the case of the Deva, but very much reduced when comparison is made with the animal jīva. Rajas has great independent activity, and sattvā is also considerably active. In the animal creation sattva has considerably less activity. Rajas has less independent activity than in man, but is much more active than in the vegetable world. Tamas is greatly less preponderant than in the latter. In the vegetable kingdom tamas is more preponderant than in the case of animals and both rajas and sattva less so. In the inorganic creation rajas makes tamas active to suppress both sattva and its own independent activity. It will thus be seen that the "upward" or revealing movement from the predominance of tamas to that of sattva represents the spiritual progress of the jīvātmā.

Again, as between each member of these classes one or other of the three guṇas may be more or less in the ascendant.

Thus, in one man as compared with another, the sattva guṇa may predominate, in which case his temperament is sāttvik, or, as the Tantra calls it, divyabhāva. In another the rajoguṇa may prevail, and in the third the tamoguṇa, in which case the individual is described as rājasik, or tāmasik, or, to use Tāntrik phraseology, he is said to belong to vīrabhāva, or is a paśu respectively. Again the vegetable creation is obviously less tāmasik and more rājasik and sāttvik than the mineral, and even amongst these last there may be possibly some which are less tāmasik than others.

Etymologically, sattva is derived from "sat," that which is eternally existent. The eternally existent is also Chit, pure Intelligence or Spirit, and ānanda or Bliss. In a secondary sense, sat is also used to denote the "good". And commonly (though such use obscures the original meaning), the word sattva guṇa is rendered "good quality." It is, however, "good" in the sense that it is productive of good and happiness. In such a case, however, stress is laid rather on a necessary quality or effect (in the ethical sense) of 'sat' than upon its original meaning. In the primary sense sat is that which reveals. Nature is a revelation of spirit (sat). Where Nature is such a revelation of spirit there it manifests as sattva guṇa. It is the shining forth from under the veil of the hidden spiritual substance (sat). And that quality in things which reveals this is sattva guṇa. So of a pregnant woman it is said that she is antahsattva, or instinct with sattva; she in whom sattva as jīva (whose characteristic guṇa is sattva) is living in a hidden state.

But Nature not only reveals, but is also a dense covering or veil of spirit, at times so dense that the ignorant fail to discern the spirit which it veils. Where Nature is a veil of spirit there it appears in its quality of tamoguṇa.

In this case the tamoguṇa is currently spoken of as representative of inertia, because that is the effect of the nature which veils. This quality, again, when translated into the moral sphere, becomes ignorance, sloth, etc.

In a third sense nature is a bridge between spirit which reveals and matter which veils. Where Nature is a bridge of descent from spirit to matter, or of ascent from matter to spirit there it manifests itself as rajoguṇa. This is generally referred to as the quality of activity, and when transferred to the sphere of feeling it shows itself as passion. Each thing in nature then contains that in which spirit is manifested or reflected as in a mirror or sattva-guṇa; that by which spirit is covered, as it were, by a veil of darkness or tamoguṇa, and that which is the vehicle for the descent into matter or the return to spirit or rajoguṇa. Thus sattva is the light of Nature, as tamas is its shade. Rajas is, as it were, a blended tint oscillating between each of the extremes constituted by the other guṇas.

The object of Tāntrik sādhana is to bring out and make preponderant the sattva guṇa by the aid of rajas, which operates to make the former guṇa active. The subtle body (lingaśarīra) of the jīvātmā comprises in it buddhi, ahangkāra, manas, and the ten senses. This subtle body creates for itself gross bodies suited to the spiritual state of the jīvātmā. Under the influence of prārabdha karma, buddhi becomes tāmasik, rājasik, or sāttvik. In the first case the jīvātmā assumes inanimate bodies; in the second, active passionate bodies; and in the third, sāttvik bodies of varying degrees of spiritual excellence, ranging from man to the Deva. The gross body is also triguṇātmaka. This body conveys impressions to the jīvātmā through the subtle body and the buddhi in particular. When sattva is made active impressions of happiness result, and when rajas or tamas are active the impressions are those of sorrow and delusion. These impressions are the result of the predominance of these respective guṇas. The action of rajas on sattva produces happiness, as its own independent activity or operation on tamas produces sorrow and delusion respectively. Where sattva or happiness is predominant, there sorrow and delusion are suppressed. Where rajas or sorrow is predominant, there happiness and delusion are suppressed. And where tamas or delusion predominates there, as in the case of the inorganic world, both happiness and sorrow are suppressed. All objects share these three states in different proportions. There is, however always in the jivātmā an admixture of sorrow with happiness, due to the operation of rajas. For happiness, which is the fruit of righteous acts done to attain happiness, is after all only a vikāra. The natural state of the jīvātmā—that is, the state of its own true nature—is that bliss (ānanda) which arises from the pure knowledge of the Self, in which both happiness and sorrow are equally objects of indifference. The worldly enjoyment of a person involves pain to self or others. This is the result of the pursuit of happiness, whether by righteous or unrighteous acts. As spiritual progress is made, the gross body becomes more and more refined. In inanimate bodies, karma operates to the production of pure delusion. On the exhausion of such karma, the jīvātmā assumes animate bodies for the operation of such forms of karma as lead to sorrow and happiness mixed with delusion. In the vegetable world, sattva is but little active, with a corresponding lack of discrimination, for discrimination is the effect of sattva in buddhi, and from discrimination arises the recognition of pleasure, and pain, conceptions of right and wrong, of the transitory and intransitory, and so forth, which are the fruit of a high degree of discrimination, or of activity of sattva. In the lower animal, sattva in buddhi is not sufficiently active to lead to any degree of development of these conceptions. In man, however, the sattva in buddhi is considerably active, and in consequence these conceptions are natural in him. For this reason the human birth is, for spiritual purposes, so important. All men, however, are not capable of forming such conceptions in an equal degree. The degree of activity in an individual's buddhi depends on his prārabdha karma. However bad such karma may be in any particular case, the individual is yet gifted with that amount[1] of discrimination

1. Corresponding to the theological doctrine of "sufficiency of grace".

which, if properly aroused and aided, will enable him to better his spiritual condition by inducing the rajoguṇa in him to give more and more activity to the sattva guṇa in his buddhi.

On this account proper guidance and spiritual direction are necessary. A good guru, by reason of his own nature and spiritual attainment and disinterested wisdom, will both mark out for the siṣya the path which is proper for him, and aid him to follow it by the infusion of the tejas which is in the Guru himself. Whilst sādhana is, as stated, a process for the stimulation of the sattva guṇa, it is evident that one form of it is not suitable to all. It must be adapted to the spiritual condition of the siṣya, otherwise it will cause injury instead of good. Therefore it is that the adoption of certain forms of sādhana by persons who are not competent (adhikārī), may not only be fruitless of any good result, but may even lead to evils which sādhana as a general principle is designed to prevent. Therefore also is it said that it is better to follow one's own dharma than that, however exalted it be, of another.

# THE WORLDS (LOKAS)

This earth, which is the object of the physical senses and of the knowledge based thereon, is but one of fourteen worlds or regions placed "above" and "below" it, of which (as the sūtra says[1]) knowledge may be obtained by meditation on the solar "nerve" (nādī) suṣumnā in the meru-daṇḍa. On this nādī six of the upper worlds are threaded, the seventh and highest overhanging it in the Sahasrāra-Padma, the thousand-petalled lotus. The sphere of earth (Bhūrloka), with its continents, their mountains and rivers, and with its oceans, is the seventh or lowest of the upper worlds. Beneath it are the Hells and Nether Worlds, the names of which are given below. Above the terrestrial sphere is Bhuvarloka, or the atmospheric sphere known as the antarikṣā, extending "from the earth to the sun," in which the Siddhas and other celestial beings (devayoni) of the upper air dwell. "From the sun to the pole star" (dhruva) is svarloka, or the heavenly sphere. Heaven (svarga) is that which delights the mind, as hell (naraka) is that which gives it pain.[2] In the former is the abode of the Deva and the blest.

---

1. Bhuvanajnānaṁ sūryye saṁyamāt, Patanjali Yoga-Sutra (chap. iii, 26). An account of the lokas is given in Vyāsa's Commentary on the sūtra, in the Viṣṇu-Purāna (Bk. II, chaps. v-vii): and in the Bhāgavata, Vāyu, and other Purāṇas.

2. Viṣṇu-Purāṇa (Bk. II·, chap. vi). Virtue is heaven and vice is hell, *ibid*, Narakamināti=kleśaṁ prāpayati, or giving pain.

These three spheres are the region of the consequences of work, and are termed transitory as compared with the three highest spheres, and the fourth, which is of a mixed character. When the jīva has received his reward he is reborn again on earth. For it is not good action, but the knowledge of the Atmā which procures Liberation (mokṣa). Above Svarloka is Maharloka, and above it the three ascending regions known as the janaloka, tapoloka, and satyaloka, each inhabited by various forms of celestial intelligence of higher and higher degree. Below the earth (Bhūh) and above[1] the nether worlds are the Hells (commencing with Avīchi), and of which, according to popular theology, there are thirty-four,[2] though it is elsewhere said[3] there are as many hells as there are offences for which particular punishments are meted out. Of these, six are known as the great hells. Hinduism, however, even when popular, knows nothing of a hell of eternal torment. To it nothing is eternal but the Brahman. Issuing from the Hells the jīva is again reborn to make its future. Below the Hells are the seven nether worlds, Sutala, Vitala, Talātala, Mahātala, Rasātala, Atala, and Pātāla, where, according to the Purāṇas, dwell the Nāga serpent divinities, brilliant with jewels, and where, too, the lovely daughters of the Daityas and Dānavas wander, fascinating even the most austere. Yet below Pātāla is the form of Viṣṇu proceeding from the dark quality (tamoguṇāh), known as the Śeṣa serpent or Ananta bearing the entire world as a diadem, attended by his Śakti Vāruṇī,[4] his own embodied radiance.

1. Ganabheda of Vahni-Purāṇa.
2. Devi-Purāṇa.
3. Viṣṇu-Purāṇa.
4. Not "the Goddess of Wine," as Wilson (Viṣṇu Pr.) has it.

## INHABITANTS OF THE WORLDS

THE worlds are inhabited by countless grades of beings, ranging from the highest Devas (of whom there are many classes and degrees) to the lowest animal life. The scale of beings runs from the shining manifestations to spirit of those in which it is so veiled that it would seem almost to have disappeared in its material covering. There is but one Light, one Spirit, whose manifestations are many. A flame enclosed in a clear glass loses but little of its brilliancy. If we substitute for the glass, paper, or some other more opaque yet transparent substance, the light is dimmer. A covering of metal may be so dense as to exclude from sight the rays of light which yet burns within with an equal brilliancy. As a fact, all such veiling forms are māyā. They are none the less true for those who live in and are themselves part of the māyik world. Deva, or "heavenly and shining one"—for spirit is light and self-manifestation—is applicable to those descending yet high manifestations of the Brahman, such as the seven Śivas, including the Trinity (trimūrti), Brahmā, Viṣṇū, and Rudra. Devī again, is the title of the Supreme Mother Herself, and is again applied to the manifold forms assumed by the one only Māyā, such as Kālī, Sarasvatī, Lakṣmi, Gaurī, Gāyatrī, Saṁdhyā, and others. In the sense also in which it is said,[1] "Verily, in the beginning there was the Brahman. It created the Devas," the latter term also

1. Bṛhadāraṇyaka Up. (ix, 2-3-2).

includes lofty intelligences belonging to the created world intermediate between Iśvara (Himself a Puruṣa) and man, who in the person of the Brāhmana is known as Earth-deva (bhūdeva).[1] These spirits are of varying degrees. For there are no breaks in the creation which represents an apparent descent of the Brahman in gradually lowered forms. Throughout these forms play the divine currents of pravṛtti and nivṛtti, the latter drawing to Itself that which the former has sent forth.[2]

Deva, jīva and jada (inorganic matter) are, in their real, as opposed to their phenomenal and illusory being, the one Brahman, which appears thus to be other than Itself through its connection with the upādhi or limiting conditions with which ignorance (avidyā) invests it. Therefore all beings which are the object of worship are each of them but the Brahman seen through the veil of avidyā. Though the worshippers of Devas may not know it, their worship is in reality the worship of the Brahman, and hence the Mahānirvāṇa-Tantra says[3] that, "as all streams flow to the ocean, so the worship given to any Deva is received by the Brahman." On the other hand, those who, knowing this, worship the Devas, do so as manifestations of the Brahman,

---

1. In like manner, the priest of the Church on earth is called by Malachi (ii. 7) "angel'", which is as Pseudo-Dionysius Areopagitae says: "From his announcement of the truth and from his desire and office of purifying, illuminating, and perfecting those committed to his charge"; the brahmanical office, in fact, when properly understood and given effect to.

2. The hierarchies have also their reason and uses in Christian theology: "Totus conatus omnium spirituum est referee Deum. Deus in primis potenter assimilat quod vicina sunt ei; assimilata deinceps assimilant. Ita pergit derivatio deitatis ab ordine in ordinem et ab hierarchia in hierarchiam et a melioribus creaturis in deteriores pro capacitate cujusque in deificationem omnium." ("Coletus de Cœlesti Hierarchia Dionysii Areopagitæ," chap. iii).

3. Chapter II, verse 50, a common statement which appears in the Bhagavadgītā and elsewhere.

and thus worship It mediately. The sun, the most glorious symbol in the physical world, is the māyik vesture of Her who is "clothed with the sun."

In the lower ranks of the celestial hierarchy are the Devayonis, some of whom are mentioned in the opening verses of the first chapter of the text. The Devas are of two classes: "unborn" (ajāta)—that is, those which have not, and those which have (sādhya) evolved from humanity as in the case of King Nahuṣa, who became Indra. Opposed to the divne hosts are the Asura, Dānavā, Daitya, Rākṣasa, who, with other spirits, represent the tāmasik or demonic element in creation. All Devas, from the highest downwards, are subordinate to both time and karma. So it is said, "Salutation to Karma, over which not even Vidhi (Brahmā) prevails" (Namastat karmmabhyovidhirapi na yebhyah prabhavati).[1] The rendering of the term "Deva" as "God"[2] has led to a misapprehension of Hindu thought. The use of the term "angel" may also mislead, for though the world of Devas has in some respects analogy to the angelic choirs,[3] the Christian conception of

---

1. And again:

Ye samasta jagatsṛṣṭisthitisamhāra kārinah
Te'pi kāleṣu līyante kālo hi balavattarah.

(Even all those who are the cause of the creation, maintenance, and destruction of the world disappear in time because time is more strong than they).

2. Though, also, as Coletus says ("De Coelesta Dionysii Hierarchia", chap. xii. 8) the Angels have been called "Gods"; "Quod autem angeli Dii vocantur testatur illud geneseos dictum Jacob a viro luctatore," etc.

3. Particularly, as I have elsewhere shown, with such conception of the celestial hieararchies as is presented by the work of the Pseudo — Dionysius on that subject written under the influence of Eastern thought (Stephen Bar Sudaili and others). As to the Christian doctrine on the Angels, see Suarez' "De Angelis." The patristic doctrine is summarised by Petavius "De Angelis," Dogm tom., III. The cabalistic names of the nine orders as given by Archangelus at p. 728 of his "Interpretationes in artis Cabalistice scriptores" (1587).

these Beings, their origin and functions, does not include, but in fact excludes, other ideas connoted by the Sanskrit term.

The pitṛs, or "Fathers," are a creation (according to some) separate from the predecessors of humanity, and are, according to others, the lunar ancestry who are addressed in prayer with the Devas. From Brahmā, who is known as the "Grandfather" Pitā Mahā of the human race, issued Marīchi, Atri, and others, his "mental sons": the Agniṣvāttāh, Saumsaya, Haviṣmantah, Uṣmapāh, and other classes of Pitṛs, numbering, according to the Mārkaṅdeya-Purāṇa, thirty-one. Tarpaṇam, or oblation, is daily offered to these pitṛs. The term is also applied to the human ancestors of the worshipper generally up to the seventh generation to whom in śrāddha (the obsequial rites) piṇda and water are offered with the mantra "svadhā".

The Ṛṣis are seers who know, and by their knowledge are the makers of Sāstra and "see" all mantras. The word comes from the root ṛṣ;[1] Ṛṣati-prāpnoti sarvaṁ mantraṁ jnānena paśyati sangsārapārangvā, etc. The seven great Ṛṣis or saptarṣis of the first manvantara are Marīci, Atri, Angiras, Pulaha, Kratu, Pulastya, and Vasiṣṭha. In other manvantaras there are other saptarṣis. In the present manvantara the seven are Kāśyapa, Atri, Vasiṣṭha, Viśvāmitra, Gautama, Jamadagṇi, Bharadvāja. To the Ṛṣis the Vedas were revealed. Vyāsa taught the Ṛgveda so revealed to Paila, the Yajurveda to Vaisampāyana, the Sāmaveda to Jaimini, Atharvāveda to Sumantu, and Itihāsa and Purāna to Sūta. The three chief classes of Ṛṣis are the Brahmarṣi, born of the mind of Brahma, the Devarṣi of lower rank, and Rājarṣi or Kings who became Ṛṣis through their knowledge and austerities, such as Janaka, Ṛtupurṇa, etc.

---

1. Śabdakalpadruma. Sub voc.

The Śrutarṣi are makers of Śāstras, as Suśruta. The Kāndarṣi are of the Karmakānda, such as Jaimini.

The Muni, who may be a Ṛṣi, is a sage. Muni is so called on account of his mananam (mananāt munirucyate). Mananam is that thought, investigation, and discussion which marks the independent thinking mind. First there is Śravanaṁ, listening; then Mananam, which is the thinking or understanding, discussion upon, and testing of what is heard as opposed to the mere acceptance on trust of the lower intelligence. These two are followed by Nididhyāsanaṁ, which is attention and profound meditation on the conclusions (siddhānta) drawn from what is so heard and reasoned upon. As the Mahābhārata says, "The Vedas differ, and so do the Smṛtis. No one is a muni who has no independent opinion of his own (nāsau muniryasya mataṁ na bhinnam)."

The human being is called jīva[1]—that is, the embodied Ātmā possessed by egoism and of the notion that it directs the puryaṣṭaka, namely, the five organs of action (karmendriya), the five organs of perception (jnānendriya), the fourfold antahkaraṇa or mental self (Manas, Buddhi, Ahaṁkāra, Citta), the five vital airs (Prāṇa), the five elements, Kāma (desire), Karma (action and its results), and Avidyā (illusion). When these false notions are destroyed, the embodiment is destroyed, and the wearer of the māyik garment attains nirvāṇa. When the jīva is absorbed in Brahman, there is no longer any jīva remaining as such.

1. That is specially so as all embodiments, whether human or not, of the Paramātmā are jiva.

## VARṆA

Ordinarily there are four chief divisions or castes (varṇa) of Hindu society—viz.: Brāhmaṇa (priesthood; teaching); Kṣattriya (warrior); Vaiśya (merchant); Śūdra (servile) -said to have spring respectively from the mouth, arm, thigh, and foot of Brahmā. A man of the first three classes becomes on investiture, during the upanayana ceremony of the sacred thread, twice-born (dvija). It is said that by birth one is śūdra, by saṁskāra (upanayana) dvija (twice-born); by study of the Vedas one attains the state of a vipra; and that he who has knowledge of the Brahman is a Brāhmaṇa.[1] The present Tantra, however, speaks of a fifth or hybrid class (sāmānya), resulting from intermixture between the others. It is a peculiarity of Tantra that its worship is largely free of Vaidik exclusiveness, whether based on caste, sex or otherwise. As the Gautamīya-Tantra says, "The Tantra is for all men, of whatever caste, and for all women" (Sarvavarṇādhikāraśca nārīṇāṁ yogya eva ca).

---

1. Janmanā jāyate Śūdrah
Saṁskārād dvija ucyate
Veda-pāthat bhavet viprah
Brahma jñānāti brāhmaṇāh.

# ĀŚRAMA

The four stages, conditions, or periods in the life of a Brāhmaṇa are: First, that of the chaste student, or brahmacārī; second, the period of secular life as a married householder or gṛhastha; third, that of the recluse, or vānaprastha, when there is retirement from the world; and lastly, that of the beggar, or bhikṣu, who begs his single daily meal, and meditates upon the Supreme Spirit to which he is about to return. For the Kṣattriya there are the first three Aśramas; for the Vaiśya, the first two; and for the Śūdra, the gṛhastha Āśrama only.[1] This Tantra[2] states that in the Kali age there are only two Āsramas. The second gārhasthya and the last bhikṣuka or avadhūta. Neither the conditions of life, nor the character, capacity, and powers of the people of this age allow of the first and third. The two āśramas prescribed for Kali age are open to all castes indiscriminately.[3]

There are, it is now commonly said, two main divisions of avadhūta — namely, Śaivāvadhūta and Brahmāvadhūta — of each of which there are, again, three divisions.[4] Of the first class the divisions are firstly

1. Yoga Yājnavalkya (chap. i).

2. Chapter VIII, verse 8.

3. *Ibid.*, verse 12.

4. Mahānirvāṇa Tantra deals with the avadhūta (those who have relinquished the world in Chapter XIV, verse 142, et· seq. The Bhairavadāmara classes the avadhūtā into (1) Kulāvadhūta, (2) Śaivāvadhūta, (3) Brāhmāvadhūta, and (4) Haṁsāvadhūta, following in the main, distinctions made in this Tantra.

Śaivāvadhūta, who is apūrṇa (imperfect). Though an ascetic, he is also a householder and like Śiva. Hence his name. The second is the wandering stage of the Śaiva (or the parivrājaka), who has now left the world, and passes his time doing pūjā, japa, etc., visiting the tīrtha and pīṭha, or places of pilgrimage. In this stage, which though higher, is still imperfect, the avadhūta is competent for ordinary sādhana with a śakti. The third is the perfect stage of a Śaiva. Wearing only the kaupīna,[1] he renounces all things and all rites, though within certain limits he may practise some yoga, and is permitted to meet the request of a woman who makes it of him.[2] Of the second class the three divisions are, firstly, the Brahmāvadhūta, who, like the Śaivāvadhūta, is imperfect (apūrna) and householder. He is not permitted, however, to have a Śaiva Śakti, and is restricted to avīyaśakti. The second class Brahma-parivrājaka is similar to the Śaiva of the same class except that ordinarily he is not permitted to have anything to do with any woman, though he may, under the guidance of his Guru, practise yoga accompanied by Śakti. The third or highest class—Haṁsāvadhūta — is similar to the third Śaiva degree, except that he must under no circumstances touch a woman or metals, nor may he practise any rites or keep any observances.

1. The exiguous loin cloth of ascetics covering only the genitals. See the Kaupīnapancakām of Śaṁkarācāryā, where the Kaupīnavān is described as the fortunate one living on the handful of rice got by begging; ever pondering upon the words of the Vedānta, whose senses are in repose, who ever enjoys the Brahman in the thought Ahambrahmāsmi.

2. This is not, however, as some may suppose, a peculiarly "Tantrik" precept, for it is said in Śruti "talpāgātāṁ na pariharet" (she who comes to your bed is not to be refused), for the rule of chastity which is binding on him yields to such an advance on the part of woman. Saṁkarācārya says that talpāgātāṁ is samāgāmarthinim, adding that this is the doctrine of Ṛṣi Vāmadeva.

## MACROCOSM AND MICROCOSM

THE universe consists of a Mahābrahmānda, or grand Kosmos, and of numerous Bṛhatbrahmānda, or macrocosms evolved from it. As is said by the Nirvāṇa-Tantra, all which is in the first is in the second. In the latter are heavenly bodies and beings, which are microcosms reflecting on a minor scale the greater worlds which evolve them. "As above, so below". This mystical maxim of the West is stated in the Viśvasāra-Tantra as follows: "What is here is elsewhere; what is not here is nowhere" (yadihāsti tadanyatra yannehāsti na tatkvacit). The macrocosm has its meru, or vertebral column, extending from top to bottom. There are fourteen regions descending from Satyaloka, the highest. These are the seven upper and the seven nether worlds (vide *ante*). The meru of the human body is the spinal column, and within it are the cakras, in which the worlds are said to dwell. In the words of the Śāktatānanda-Taranginī, they are piṇdamadhyesthitā. Satya has been said to be in the sahasrārā, and Tapah, Janah, Mahah, Svah, Bhuvah, Bhūh in the ājnā, viśuddhi, anāhata, maṇipūra, svādhisthāna, and mūlādhāra lotuses respectively. Below mūlādhāra and in the joints, sides, anus, and organs of generation are the nether worlds. The bones near the spinal column are the kula-parvata.[1] Such

1. The seven main chains of mountains in Bhārata (see Viṣṇu-Purāṇa, Bk. II, chap. iii).

are the correspondences as to earth. Then as to water. The nādīs are the rivers. The seven substances of the body (dhātu)[1] are the seven islands. Sweat, tears, and the like are the oceans. Fire exists in the mūlādhāra, suṣumnā, navel, and elsewhere.[2] As the worlds are supported by the prāṇa and other vāyus ("airs"), so is the body supported by the ten vāyus, prāna, etc. There is the same ākāśa (ether) in both.[3] The witness within is the puruṣa without, for the personal soul of the microcosm corresponds to the cosmic soul (hiraṇyagarbha) in the macrocosm.

---

1. Skin, blood. muscle, tendon, bone, fat, semen.

2. The kāmāgni in mūlādhāra, badala in the bones; in suṣumnā, the fire of lightning, and in the navel earthly fire.

3. As to distribution of elements in the cakras, see chap. iv, Bhūtaśuddhi-Tantra.

## THE AGES

THE passage of time within a mahā-yuga influences for the worse man and the world in which he lives. This passage is marked by the four ages (yuga), called Satya, Treta, Dvāpara, and Kali-yuga, the last being that in which it is generally supposed the world now is. The yuga[1] is a fraction of a kalpa, or day of Brahmā of 4,320,000,000 years. The kalpa is divided into fourteen manvantaras, which are again subdivided into seventy-one mahā yuga; the length of each of which is 4,320,000 human years. The mahā-yuga (great age) is itself composed of four yugas (ages)—(*a*) Satya, (*b*) Treta, (*c*) Dvāpara (*d*) Kali. Official science teaches that man appeared on the earth in an imperfect state, from which he has since been gradually, though continually, raising himself. Such teaching is, however, in conflict with the traditions of all peoples—Jew, Babylonian, Egyptian, Hinḍu, Greek, Roman, and Christian —which speak of an age when man was both innocent and happy. From this state of primal perfection he fell, continuing his descent until such time as the great Avatāras, Christ and others, descended to save his race and enable it to regain the righteous path. The Garden of Eden is the emblem of the paradisiacal body of man. There man was one with Nature. He was himself paradise, a privileged enclosure in a garden of delight[2]—gan be Eden. Et eruditus

---

1. See Bentley, "Hindu Astronomy" (1828), p. 10.

2. Genesis ii. 8: Paradise is commonly confused with Eden, but the two are different. Paradise is in Eden.

est Moyse omni sapientia Ægyptiorum. The Satya Yuga is, according to Hindu belief, the Golden Age of righteousness, free of sin, marked by longevity, physical strength, beauty, and stature. "There were giants in those days" whose moral, mental, and physical strength enabled them to undergo long brahmacarya (continence) and tapas (austerities). Longevity permitted lengthy spiritual exercises. Life then depended on the marrow, and lasted a lakh of years'[1] men dying when they willed. Their stature was 21 cubits.

To this age belong the Avatāras or incarnations of Viṣnu, Matsya, Kūrma, Varāha, Nṛ-siṁha, and Vāmana, Its duration is computed to be 4,800 Divine years, which, when multiplied by 360 (a year of the Devas being equal to 360 human years) are the equivalent of 1,728,000 of the years of man. (b) The second age, or Tretā (three-fourth) Yuga, is that in which righteousness (dharma) decreased by one-fourth. The duration was 3,600 Divine years, or 1,296,000 human years. Longevity, strength, and stature decreased. Life was in the bone, and lasted 10,000 years. Man's stature was 14 cubits. Of sin there appeared one-quarter, and of virtue there remained three-quarters. Men were still attached to pious and charitable acts, penances, sacrifice, and pilgrimage, of which the chief was that to Naimiśāraṇya. In this period appeared the avatāras of Viṣṇu as Paraśurāma and Rāma. (c) The third, or Dvāpara (one-half) yuga, is that in which righteousness decreased by one-half, and the duration was 2,400 Divine, or 864,000 human years. A further decrease in longevity and strength, and increase of weakness and disease mark this age. Life which lasted 1,000 years was centred in the blood. Stature

---

1. Cf. the Biblical account of the long-lived patriarchs, Methuselah and others: and for more favourable modern estimate of the "Primitives," see M. A. Leblond, "L'Ideal du dīxneuvīēme siēcle," and Elie Reclus' celebrated work on the Primitives (1888).

was 7 cubits. Sin and virtue were of equal force. Men became restless, and though eager to acquire knowledge, were deceitful, and followed both good and evil pursuits. The principal place of pilgrimage was Kurukṣetra. To this age belongs (according to Vyāsa, Anuṣṭubhācārya and Jaya-deva) the avatāra of Viṣṇu as Bala-rāma, the elder brother of Kṛṣṇa, who, according to other accounts, takes his place. In the saṁdhya, or intervening period of 1,000 years between this and the next yuga the Tantra was revealed, as it will be revealed at the dawn of every Kali-yuga. (d) Kali-yuga is the alleged present age, in which righteousness exists to the extent of one-fourth only, the duration of which is 1,200 Divine, or 432,000 human years. According to some, this age commenced in 3120 B.C. on the date of Viṣṇu's return to heaven after the eighth incarnation. This is the period which, according to the Purāṇas and Tantras, is characterized by the prevalence of viciousness, weakness, disease, and the general decline of all that is good. Human life, which lasts at most 120, or, as some say, 100, years, is dependent on food. Stature is 3½ cubits. The chief pilgrimage is now to the Ganges. In this age has appeared the Buddha Avatāra. The last, or Kalki Avatāra, the Destroyer of sin, has yet to come. It is He who will destroy iniquity and restore the age of righteousness. The Kalki-Purāṇa speaks of Him as one whose body is blue like that of the rain-charged cloud, who with sword in hand rides, as does the rider of the Apocalypse, a white horse swift as the wind, the Cherisher of the people, Destroyer of the race of the Kali-yuga, the source of true religion. And Jayadeva, in his Ode to the Incarnations, addresses Him thus: For the destruction of all the impure thou drawest thy scimitar like a blazing comet. O how tremendous! Oh, Keśava, assuming the body of

Kalki; Be victorious, O Hari, Lord of the Universe!" With the satya-yuga a new mahā-yuga will commence and the ages will continue to revolve with their rising and descending races until the close of the kalpa or day of Brahmā. Then a night of dissolution (pralaya) of equal duration follows, the Lord reposing in yoga-nidrā (yoga sleep in pralaya) on the Serpent Śeṣa, the Endless One, till daybreak, when the universe is created anew and the next kalpa follows.

## THE SCRIPTURES OF THE AGES

EACH of these Ages has its appropriate Śāstra or Scripture, designed to meet the characteristics and needs of the men who live in them.[1] The Hindu Śāstras are classed into: (1) Śruti, which commonly includes the four Vedas (Ṛik, Yajuh, Sāma, Atharva) and the Upaniṣads, the doctrine of which is philosophically exposed in the Vedānta-Darśana. (2) Smṛti, such as the Dharma Śāstra of Manu and other works on family and social duty prescribing for pravṛtti-dharma, as the Upaniṣads had revealed the nivṛtti-dharma. (3) The Purāṇas,[2] of which, according to the Brahma-vaivarta Purāṇa, there were originally four lakhs, and of which eighteen are now regarded as the principal. (4) The Tantra.

For each of these ages a suitable Śāstra is given. The Veda is the root of all Śāstras (mula-śāstra). All others are based on it. The Tantra is spoken of as a fifth Veda. Kulluka-Bhatta, the celebrated commentator on Manu, says that Śruti is of two kinds, Vaidik and Tāntrik (vaidikī-tāntrikī caiva dvi-vidha śrutih-kīrtitā). The

---

1. Of the subject matter of this paragraph see my Introduction to "The Principles of Tantra" (Tantra-tattva), where it is dealt with in greater detail.

2. These are referred to as saṁhitā (collection), which term includes amongst other things Dharma-Śāstra, Smṛti, Śrutijīvikā, Purāṇas, Upa-purāṇās, Itihāsa (history), the books of Vasiṣtha, Vālmīkī, and others. See Śabda-ratnāvali, and Brahmavaivartta Purāṇa, Jnāna-Kāṇda, chap. cxxxii.

various Śāstras, however, are different presentments of śruti appropriate to the humanity of the age for which they are given. Thus the Tantra is that presentment of śruti which is modelled as regards its ritual to meet the characteristics and infirmities of the Kali-yuga. As men have no longer the capacity, longevity, and moral strength necessary for the application of the Vaidika Karma-kāṇḍa, the Tantra prescribes a special sādhana, or means or practice of its own, for the attainment of that which is the ultimate and common end of all Śāstras. The Kulārṇava-Tantra says[1] that in the Satya or Kṛta age the Śāstra is Śruti (in the sense of the Veda and Upaniṣads); in Tretā-yuga, Smṛti (in the sense of the Dharma-Śāstra and Śruti-jīvikā, etc.); in the Dvāpara Yuga, the Purāṇa; and in the last or Kali-yuga, the Tantra, which should now be followed by all orthodox Hindu worshippers. The Mahānirvāṇa[2] and other Tantras and Tāntrik works[3] lay down the same rule. The Tantra is also said to contain the very core of the Veda to which, it is described to bear the relation of the Paramātmā to the Jīvātmā. In a similar way, Kulācāra is the central informing life of the gross body called vedācāra, each of the ācāra which follow it up to kaulācāra, being more and more subtle sheaths.

---

1. Kṛte śrutyukta ācārastretāyāṁ smṛtī-saṁbhavāḥ, Dvāpare tu purāṇoktaṁ kalau āgama kevalaṁ.

2. Chapter I, verse 23 et seq.

3. So the Tārā-pradīpa (chap. i) says that in the Kali-yuga the Tāntrika and not the Vaidika-Dharma is to be followed (see as to the Śāstras, my Introduction to "Principles of Tantra").

## THE HUMAN BODY

THE human body is Brahma-pura, the city of Brahman. Iśvara Himself enters into the universe as jīva. Wherefore the mahā-vākya "That thou art" means that the ego (which is regarded as jīva only from the standpoint of an upādhi[1]) is Brahman.

## THE FIVE SHEATHS

In the body there are five kośas or sheaths—anna-maya, prāṇa-maya, mano-maya, vijnāna-maya, ānanda-maya, or the physical and vital bodies, the two mental bodies, and the body of bliss.[2] In the first the Lord is self-conscious as being dark or fair, short or tall, old or youthful. In the vital body He feels alive, hungry, and thirsty. In the mental bodies He thinks and understands. And in the body of Bliss He resides in happiness. Thus garmented with the five garments, the Lord, though all-pervading, appears as though He were limited by them.[3]

---

1. An apparently conditioning limitation of the Absolute.

2. According to "Theosophic" teaching, the first two sheaths are apparently the physical body in its dense (Anna-maya) and etheric (Prána-maya) forms. Mano-maya represents the astral (Kāma) and lower mental body; Vijnāna-maya the higher mental or (theosophical) causal body, and the highest the Ātmik body.

3. Mānasollāsa of Sureśvarācārya, Commentary on third śloka of the Dakṣinā-mūrtī-stotra.

## ANNA-MAYA KOŚA

In the material body, which is called the "sheath of food" (anna-maya kośa), reign the elements earth, water, and fire, which are those presiding in the lower Cakras, the Mūlādhāra, Svādhiṣthānā, and Mani-purā centres. The two former produce food and drink, which is assimilated by the fire of digestion, and converted into the body of food. The indriyas are both the faculty and organs of sense. There are in this body the material organs, as distinguished from the faculty of sense.

In the gross body (śarīra-kośa) there are six external kośas—viz., hair, blood, flesh,[1] which come from the mother, and bone, muscle, marrow, from the father.

The organs of sense (indriya) are of two kinds—viz.: jnānendriyas or organs of sensation, through which knowledge of the external world is obtained (ear, skin, eyes, tongue, nose); and karmendriya or organs of action, mouth, arms, legs, anus, penis, the functions of which are speech, holding, walking, excretion, and procreation.

## PRĀNA-MAYA KOŚA

The second sheath is the prāṇa-maya-kośa, or sheath of "breath" (prāṇa), which manifests itself in air and ether, the presiding elements in the Anāhata and Viśuddha-cakras.

There are ten vāyus (airs), or inner vital forces, of which the first five[2] are the principal—namely, the sapphire prāṇa; apāna the colour of an evening cloud; the silver vyāna, udāna, the colour of fire; and the milky samāna.[2]

---

1. The Prapānca-sāra (chap. ii) gives shukla (semen) instead of māṁsa (flesh).

2. See Sāradā tīlaka. The minor vāyus are nāga, kūrma, kṛkarā, devadatta, dhanaṁjayā, producing hiccup, closing and opening eyes, assistance to digestion, yawning, and distension, "which leaves not even the corpse."

These are all aspects of the action of the one Prāṇa-devata. Kuṇḍalinī is the Mother of prāṇa, which She, the Mūla-Prakṛti, illumined by the light of the Supreme Ātmā generates. Prāṇa is vāyu, or the universal force of activity, divided on entering each individual into five-fold function. Specifically considered, prāṇa is inspiration, which with expiration is from and to a distance of eight and twelve inches respectively. Udāna is the ascending vāyu. Apāna is the downward vāyu, expelling wind, excrement, urine, and semen. The samāna, or collective vāyu, kindles the bodily fire, "conducting equally the food, etc., throughout the body." Vyāna is the separate vāyu, effecting division and diffusion. These forces cause respiration, excretion, digestion, circulation.

## MANO-MAYA, VIJNĀNA- AND ĀNANDA-MAYA KOŚAS

The next two sheaths are the mano-maya and vijnāna kośas. These constitute the antah-karaṇa, which is four-fold—namely, the mind in its two-fold aspect of Buddhi and manas, self-hood (ahaṁkāra), and chitta.[1] The function of the first is doubt, saṁkalpa-vikalpātmaka, (uncertainty, certainty); of the second, determination (niscaya-kārni); of the third (egoity), consciousness (abhimāna). Manas automatically registers the facts which the senses perceive. Buddhi, on attending to such registration, discriminates, determines, and cognizes the object registered, which is set over and against the subjective self by Ahaṁkāra. The function of chitta is contemplation (chintā), the faculty[2] whereby the mind in its widest sense raises for itself the

---

1. According to Sāṁkhya, chitta is included in buddhi. The above is the Vedāntic classification.

2. The most important from the point of view of worship on account of mantra-smarana, devatā-smarana, etc.

subject of its thought and dwells thereon. For whilst buddhi has but three moments in which it is born, exists, and dies, chitta endures.

The antah-karaṇa is master of the ten senses, which are the outer doors through which it looks forth upon the external world. The faculties, as opposed to the organs or instruments of sense, reside here. The centres of the powers inherent in the last two sheaths are in the Ājnā Cakra and the region above this and below the sahasrāra lotus. In the latter the Ātmā of the last sheath of bliss resides. The physical or gross body is called sthūla-śarīra. The subtle body (śūkṣma-śarīra also called linga śarīra and karāṇa-śarīra) comprises the ten indriyas, manas, ahaṁkāra, buddhi, and the five functions of praṇa. This subtle body contains in itself the cause of rebirth into the gross body when the period of reincarnation arrives.

The ātmā, by its association with the upādhis, has three states of consciousness—namely, the jāgrat, or waking state, when through the sense organs are perceived objects of sense through the operation of manas and buddhi. It is explained in the Iśvara-pratya-bhijnā as follows — "the waking state dear to all is the source of external action through the activity of the senses." The Jīva is called jāgari—that is, he who takes upon himself the gross body called Viśva. The second is svapna, the dream state, when the sense organs being withdrawn, Ātmā is conscious of mental images generated by the impressions of jāgrat experience. Here manas ceases to record fresh sense impressions, and it and buddhi work on that which manas has registered in the waking state. The explanation of this state is also given in the work last cited. "The state of svapna is the objectification of visions perceived in the mind, due to the perception of ideas there latent." Jīva in the state of svapna is termed taijasa. Its individuality is merged in the subtle body. Hiraṇya-garbha is the collective form of these jīvas, as Vaiśvānara is such form of the jīva in the waking state. The third state is that of suśupti, or dreamless sleep, when manas itself is withdrawn, and buddhi, dominated by tamas, preserves only the notion: "Happily I slept; I was not conscious of anything" (Pātanjala-yoga-sūtra). In the macrocosm the upādhi of these states are also called Virāṭ, Hiraṇyagarbha, and Avyakta. The description of the state of sleep is given in the Śiva-sūtra as that in which there is incapacity of discrimination or illusion. By the saying cited from the Pātanjala-sūtra three modifications of avidyā are indicated—viz., ignorance, egoism, and happiness. Sound sleep is that in which these three exist. The person in that state is termed prājna, his individuality being merged in the causal body (kāraṇa). Since in the sleeping state the prājna becomes Brahman, he is no longer jīva as before; but the jīva is then not the supreme one (Paramātmā), because the state is associated with avidyā. Hence, because the vehicle in the jīva in the sleeping state is Kāraṇa, the vehicle of the jīva in the fourth is declared to be mahā-kāraṇa. Iśvara is the collective form of the prājna jīva.

Beyond suṣupti is the turīya, and beyond turīya the transcendent fifth state without name. In the fourth state śuddha-vidya is required, and this is the only realistic one for the yogī which he attains through samādhi-yoga. Jīva in turīya is merged in the great causal body (mahā-kāraṇa). The fifth state arises from firmness in the fourth. He who is in this state becomes equal to Śiva, or, more strictly tends to a close equality; for it is only beyond that, that "the spotless one attains the highest equality," which is unity. Hence even in the fourth and fifth states there is an absence of full perfection which constitutes the Supreme. Bhāskararāyā, in his Commentary on the Lalitā, when pointing out that the Tāntrik theory adds the fourth and fifth states to the first three adopted by the followers of the Upaniṣads, says that the latter states are not separately enumerated by them owing to the absence in those two states of the full perfection of Jīva or of Śiva.

## NĀDĪ

It is said[1] that there are 3½ crores of nādīs in the human body, of which some are gross and some are subtle. Nādī means a nerve or artery in the ordinary sense; but all the nādīs of which the books on Yoga[2] speak are not of this physical character, but are subtle channels of energy. Of these nādīs, the principal are fourteen; and of these fourteen, idā, pingalā and suṣumnā are the chief; and, again, of these three, suṣumna is the greatest, and to it all others are subordinate. Suṣumnā is in the hollow of the meru in the cerebro-spinal axis.[3] It extends from the Mūlādhāra lotus, the Tattvik earth centre,[4] to the cerebral region. Suṣumnā is in the form of Fire (vahni-svarūpa), and has within it the vajrini-nādī in the form of the sun (sūrya-svarūpā). Within the latter is the pale nectar-dropping

---

1. Nādī-vijnāna (chap. i, verses 4 and 5).

2. Ṣat-chakra-nirūpaṇa (commentary on verse 1), quoting from Bhūta-śuddhi-Tantra, speaks of 72000 nādis (see also Niruttara-Tantra, Prāṇa-toṣinī, p. 35), and the Śiva-saṁhitā (2, 13) of three lacs and 50,000

3. It has been thought, on the authority of the Tantra-cūdā-maṇi, that suṣumnā is outside meru; but this is not so, as the Author of the Ṣat-cakra-nirūpaṇa points out (verse 2). Iḍa and Pingalā are outside the meru; the quoted passage in Nigama-tattva-sāra referring to suṣumnā, vajrā and chitrinī.

4. The Tattvas of "earth," "water," "fire," "air," and "ether," are not to be identified with the so-called popular "elements" of those names.

citrā or citrinī nādī, which is also called Brahma-nādī, in the form of the moon (candra-svarūpā). Suṣumnā is thus triguṇā. The various lotuses in the different Cakras of the body (vide *post*) are all suspended from the citrā-nādī, the cakras being described as knots in the nādī, which is as thin as the thousandth part of hair. Outside the meru and on each side of suṣumnā are the nādīs idā and pingalā. Idā is on the left side, and coiling round suṣumnā, has its exit in the left nostril. Pingalā is on the right, and, similary coiling, enters the right nostril. The suṣumnā, interlacing idā and pingalā and the ājnā-cakra round which they pass, thus form a representation of the caduceus of Mercury. Idā is of a pale colour, is moon-like (candra-svarūpa), and contains nectar. Pingalā is red, and is sun-like (sūrya-svarūpā), containing "venom," the fluid of mortality. These three "rivers," which are united at the ājnā-cakra, flow separately from that point, and for this reason the ājnā-cakra is called muktā triveni. The mūlādhāra is called Yuktā (united), tri-veni, since it is the meeting-place of the three nādīs which are also called Gangā (Idā), Yamunā (Pingalā), and Sarasvati (suṣumnā), after the three sacred rivers of India. The opening at the end of the suṣumnā in the mūlādhāra is called brahma-dvāra, which is closed by the coils of the sleeping Devī Kuṇḍalinī.

## CAKRAS

There are six cakras, or dynamic Tattvik centres, in the body—viz., the mūlādhāra, svādhiṣṭhāna, maṇi-pūra, anāhata, viśuddha, and ājñā—which are described in the following notes. Over all these is the thousand-petalled lotus (sahasrāra-padma).

## MŪLĀDHĀRA

Mūlādhāra[1] is a triangular space in the midmost portion of the body, with the apex turned downwards like a young girl's yoni. It is described as a red lotus of four petals, situate between the base of the sexual organ and the anus. "Earth" evolved from "water" is the Tattva of the cakra. On the four petals are the four golden varṇas—"vaṁ" (वं), "śaṁ" (शं), "ṣaṁ" (षं), and "saṁ" (सं).[2] In the four petals pointed towards the four directions (Iśāna, etc.) are the four forms of bliss—yogānanda (yoga bliss), paramānanda (supreme bliss), sahajānanda (natural bliss), and vīrānanda (vīra bliss). In the centre of this lotus is Svayambhū-linga, ruddy brown, like the colour of a young leaf. Citriṇī-nādī is figured as a tube, and the opening at its end at the base of the linga is called the door of Brahman (Brahma-dvāra), through which the Devī ascends.[3] The lotus, linga and brahma-dvāra, hang downwards. The Devī Kuṇḍalinī, more subtle than the fibre of the lotus, and luminous as lightning, lies asleep coiled like a serpent around the linga, and closes with Her body the door of Brahman. The Devī has forms in the brahmāṇda. Her subtlest form in the piṇḍāṇḍa, or body, is called Kuṇḍalinī, a form of Prakṛti pervading, supporting, and expressed in

---

1. Mūla, the root; ādhāra, support; for the mūlādhāra is the root of Suṣumna and that on which Kuṇḍalinī rests.

2. It need hardly be said that it is not supposed that there are any actual lotuses or letters engraved thereon. These and other terms are employed to represent realities of yoga experience. Thus the lotus is a plexus of nādīs, the disposition of the latter at the particular cakra in question determining the number of the petals.

3. Hence She is called in the Lālitā-sahasra-nāma (verse 106) Mūlādhārāṁ-bujārūdhā.

the form of the whole universe; "the Glittering Dancer" (as the Śāradātilaka calls Her) "in the lotus-like head of the yogi." When awakened, it is She who gives birth to the world made of mantra.[1] A red fiery triangle surrounds svayaṁbhū-linga, and within the triangle is the red Kandarpa-vāyu, or air, of Kāma, a form of the apāna vāyu, for here is the seat of creative desire. Outside the triangle is a yellow square, called the pṛthivi-(earth)-maṇḍala, to which is attached the "eight thunders" (aṣta-vajra). Here is the bīja "laṁ" (ळ), and with it pṛthivi on the back of an elephant. Here also are Brahmā and Sāvitrī,[2] and the red four-handed Śakti Dākinī.[3]

## SVĀDHIṢṬHĀNA

Svādhiṣṭhāna is a six-petalled lotus at the base of the sexual organ, above mūlādhāra and below the navel. Its pericarp is red, and its petals are like lightning. "Water" evolved from "fire" is the Tattva of this cakra. The varṇas on the petals are "baṁ" (बं), "bhaṁ" (भं), "maṁ" (म), "yaṁ" (यं), "raṁ" (रं), and "laṁ" (ळं). In the six petals are also the vṛttis (states, qualities, functions or inclinations)—namely, praśraya (credulity), a-viśvāsa (suspicion, mistrust), avajnā (disdain), mūrchchā (delusion, or, as some say, disinclination), sarva-nāśa (false knowledge),[4] and krūratā (pitilessness). Within a semicircular

1. See Prāṇa-toṣinī, p. 45.

2. The Devī is Sāvitrī as wife of the Creator, who is called Savitā because He creates beings.

3. Who, according to the Sammohana-Tantra (chap. ii), acts as keeper of the door.

4. Lit. "destruction of everything," which false knowledge leads to.

space in the pericarp are the Devatā, the dark blue Mahā-viṣṇu, Mahālakṣmī, and Saraswatī. In front is the blue four-handed Rākinī Śakti, and the bījā of Varuṇa, Lord of water or "vaṁ" (वं). Inside the bīja there is the region of Varuṇa, of the shape of an half-moon, and in it is Varuṇa himself seated on a white alligator (makara).

## MANI-PŪRA

Maṇi-pūra-cakra[1] is a ten-petalled golden lotus, situate above the last in the region of the navel. "Fire" evolved from "air" is the Tattva of the cakra. The ten petals are of the colours of a cloud, and on them are the blue varṇas—"ḍaṁ" (डं), "ḍhaṁ" (ढं), "ṇaṁ" (णं), "taṁ" (तं), "thaṁ" (थं), "daṁ (दं), "dhaṁ" (धं), "naṁ" (नं), "paṁ" (पं), "phaṁ" (फं), —and the ten vṛttis (vide *ante*), namely, lajjā (shame), piśunata (fickleness), īrṣā (jealousy), tṛṣnā (desire), suṣupti (laziness),[2] viṣāda (sadness), kaṣāya (dullness), moha (ignorance), ghṛṇā (aversion, disgust), bhaya (fear). Within the pericarp is the bīja रं ("raṁ"), and a triangular figure (maṇḍala) of Agni, Lord of Fire, to each side of which figure are attached three auspicious signs or svastikas. Agni, red, four-handed, and seated on a ram, is within the figure. In front of him are Rudra and his Śakti Bhadra-kālī. Rudra is of the colour of vermilion, and is old. His body is smeared with ashes. He has three eyes and two hands. With one of these he makes the sign which grants boons and blessings,

---

1. So-called, it is said by some, because during samaya worship the Devī is (pūra) with gems (maṇī): see Bhāskara-rāya's Commentary on Lalitā-sahasra-nāma, verses 37 and 38. By others it is so called because (due to the presence of fire) it is like a gem.

2. Deeply so, with complete disinclination to action: absence of all energy

and with the other that which dispels fear. Near him is the four-armed Lākinī-Śakti of the colour of molten gold (tapta-kāncana), wearing yellow raiments and ornaments. Her mind is maddened with passion (mada-matta-citta). Above the lotus is the abode and region of Sūrya. The solar region drinks the nectar which drops from the region of the Moon.

## ANĀHATA

Anāhata-cakra is a deep red lotus of twelve petals, situate above the last and in the region of the heart, which is to be distinguished from the heart-lotus facing upwards of eight petals, spoken of in the text, where the patron deity (Iṣta-devata) is meditated upon. "Air" evolved from "ether" is the Tattva of the former lotus. On the twelve petals are the vermilion varṇas—"Kaṁ" (कं). "Khaṁ" (खं), "Gaṁ" (गं), "Ghaṁ" (घं), "ngaṁ" (ङं), "caṁ" (चं), "Chaṁ" (छं), "Jaṁ" (जं), "Jhaṁ" (झं), ñam" (ञं), "Ṭaṁ" (टं), "Thaṁ" (ठं), and the twelve vṛttis (vide *ante*)—namely, āśa(hope), chinta (care, anxiety), ceṣtā (endeavour), mamatā (sense of mineness),[1] ḍaṁbha (arrogance or hypocrisy), vikalatā (langour), ahaṁkāra (conceit), viveka (discrimination), lolatā (covetousness), kapaṭata (duplicity) vitarka (indecision), anutāpa (regret). A triangular maṇḍala within the pericarp of this lotus of the lustre of lightning is known as the Tri-kona Śakti. Within this maṇḍala is a red bāna-linga, called Nārāyaṇa or Hiraṇyagarbha, and near it Iśvara and His Sakti Bhuvaneś-vari. Iśvara, who is the Overlord of the first three cakras is of the colour of molten gold, and with His two

1. Resulting in attachment.

hands grants blessings and dispels fear. Near him is the three-eyed Kākini-Śakti, lustrous as lightning, with four hands holding the noose and drinking-cup, and making the sign of blessing, and that which dispels fear. She wears a garland of human bones. She is excited, and her heart is softened with wine. Here, also, are several other Śaktis, such as Kāla-rātri, as also the bīja of air (vāyu) or "yaṁ" (यं). Inside the lotus is a six-cornered smoke-coloured maṇḍala, and the circular region of smoke-coloured Vāyu, who is seated on a black antelope. Here, too, is the embodied ātmā (jīvātmā), like the tapering flame of a lamp.

## VIŚUDDHA

Viśuddha-cakra or Bhāratiṣthāna, abode of the Devī of speech, is above the last and at the lower end of the throat (kaṇṭha-mūla). The Tattva of this cakra is "ether". The lotus is of a smoky colour, or the colour of fire seen through smoke. It has sixteen petals, which carry the red vowels—"aṁ" (अं), "āṁ" (आं), "iṁ" (इं), "īṁ" (ईं), "uṁ" (उं), "ūṁ" (ऊं), "ṛṁ" (ऋं), "ṝṁ" (ॠं) "ḷṁ" (ऌं), "ḹṁ" (ॡं), "eṁ" (एं), "aiṁ" (ऐं) "oṁ" (ओं), "auṁ" (औं), "aṁ" (अं), "aḥ" (अः); the seven musical notes (niṣāda, ṛṣabha, gāndhāra, ṣadja, madhyama dhaivata and pancama): "venom" (in the eighth petal); the bījas "huṁ", "phat", "vauṣat". "vaṣat", "svadhā", "svāhā", "namah", and in the sixteenth petal nectar (amṛta). In the pericarp is a triangular region, within which is the androgyne Śiva, known as Ardhanārīśvara. There also are the regions of the full moon and ether, with its bīja "ham" (हं). The ākāsa-maṇḍala is transparent and round in shape. Ākāsa himself is here dressed in white, and mounted on a white elephant. He has four hands, which hold the noose[1] (pāśa), the elephant-hook[2] (aṇkuśa), and with the other he makes the mudrās which grant blessing and dispels fear. Śiva is white, with five faces, three eyes, ten arms, and is dressed in tiger skins. Near Him is the white Śakti Śākini, dressed in yellow raiments, holding in Her four hands the bow, the arrow, the noose, and the hook.

Above the cakra, at the root of the palate (tālumūla) is a concealed cakra, called Lalanā and, in some Tantras, Kalā-cakra. It is a red lotus with twelve petals, bearing the following vṛttis:—śraddhā (faith), santosha (contentment), aparādha (sense of error), dama (self-command), māna[3] (anger), sneha (affection),[4] śoka (sorrow, grief), kheda (dejection), śuddhatā (purity), arati (detachment), sambhrama (agitation),[5] Urmi (appetite, desire).

## ĀJÑĀ

Ājñā-cakra is also called parama-kula and muktā-triveṇī, since it is from here that the three nādīs—Idā, Piṅgala and suṣumnā—go their separate ways. It is a two-petalled lotus, situate between the two eyebrows. In this cakra there is no gross Tattva, but subtle Tattva mind is here. Hakārārdha, or half the letter Ha, is also there. On its petals are the red varṇas "haṁ" and "kṣaṁ".

---

1. The Devi herself holds the noose of desire. Desire is the vāsanā form and the noose is the gross form (see next note).

2. The Vāmakeśvara-Tantra says: "The noose and the elephant-hook of Her are spoken of as desire and anger. But the Yoginī-hṛdaya i. 53 says: "The noose is ichchāśakti, the goad jnāna-śakti, and the bow and arrows kriya-śakti."

3. Generally applied to the case of anger between two persons who are attached to one another, as in the case of man and wife.

4. Towards those younger or lower than oneself.

5. Through respect.

In the pericarp is concealed the bīja "oṁ". In the two petals and the pericarp there are the three guṇas—sattva, rajas and tamas. Within the triangular maṇḍala in the pericarp there is the lustrous (tejō-maya) linga in the form of the praṇava (praṇavākṛti), which is called Itara. Para-Śiva in the form of haṁsa (haṁsa-rūpa) is also there with his Śakti—Siddha-Kāli. In the three corners of the triangle are Brahmā, Viṣṇu, and Maheśvara, respectively. In this cakra there is the white Hākini-Śakti, with six heads and four hands, in which are jñāna-mudra,[1] a skull, a drum (damaru), and a rosary.

## SAHASRĀRA PADMA

Above the ājñā-cakra there is another secret cakra called manas-cakra. It is a lotus of six petals, on which are Śabda-jñāna, sparśa-jñāna, rūpa-jñāna, āghraṇopalabdhi, rasopabhoga, and svapna, or the faculties of hearing, touch, sight, smell, taste, and sleep, or the absence of these. Above this, again, there is another secret cakra, called Soma-cakra. It is a lotus of sixteen petals, which are also called sixteen Kalās.[2] These Kalās are called kṛpā (mercy), mṛdutā (gentleness), dhairya (patience, composure), vairāgya (dispassion), dhṛti (constancy), sampat (prosperity),[3] hāsya (cheerfulness), romāñca (rapture, thrill), vinaya (sense of propriety, humility), dhyāna (meditation), susthiratā (quietitude, restfulness), gāmbhīrya (gravity),[4] udyama (enterprise, effort), akṣobha (emotionlessness),[5] audārya (magnanimity), and ekāgratā (concentration).

---

1. The gesture in which the first finger is uplifted and the others closed.
2. Kalā—a part, also a digit of the moon.
3. That is, spiritual prosperity.
4. Of demeanour evidencing a grave nature.
5. The State of being undisturbed by one's emotions.

Above this last cakra is "the house without support" (nirālamba-purī), where yogis see the radiant Iśvara. Above this is the praṇava shining like a flame and above praṇava the white crescent Nāda, and above this last the point Bindu. There is then a white lotus of twelve petals with its head upwards, and over this lotus there is the ocean of nectar (sudhā-sāgara), the island of gems (maṇi-dvīpa), the altar of gems (maṇi-pītha), the forked lightning-like lines a, ka, tha, and therein Nāda and Bindu. On Nāda and Bindu, as an altar, there is the Paramahaṁsa, and the latter serves as an altar for the feet of the Guru; there the Guru of all should be meditated. The body of the Haṁsa on which the feet of the Guru rest is jñāna-maya, the wings Āgama and Nigama, the two feet Śiva and Śakti, the beak Praṇava, the eyes and throat Kāma-Kalā.

Close to the thousand-petalled lotus is the sixteenth digit of the moon, which is called amā kalā, which is pure red and lustrous like lightning, as fine as a fibre of the lotus, hanging downwards, receptacle of the lunar nectar. In it is the crescent nirvāṇa-kalā, luminous as the Sun, and finer than the thousandth part of a hair. This is the Iṣṭa-devatā of all. Near nirvāṇa-kalā is parama-nirvāṇa-Śakti, infinitely subtle, lustrous as the Sun, creatrix of tattva-jñāna. Above it are Bindu and Visarga-Śakti, root and abode of all bliss.

Sahasrāra-padma—or thousand-petalled lotus of all colours—hangs with its head downwards from the brahma-randhra above all the cakras. This is the region of the first cause (Brahma-loka), the cause of the six preceding causes. It is the great Sun both cosmically and individually, in whose effulgence Parama-Śiva and Ādyā-Śakti reside. The power is the vācaka-Śakti or saguṇa brahman, holding potentially within itself, the gunas, powers, and planes. Parama-Śiva is in the form of the Great Ether (paramākāśa-rūpī), the Supreme Spirit (paramātma), the Sun of the darkness of ignorance. In each of the petals of the lotus are placed all the letters of the alphabet; and whatever there is in the lower cakra or in the universe (brahmāṇda) exists here in potential state (avyakta-bhāva). Śaivas call this place Śiva-sthāna, Vaiṣṇavās, Parama-puruṣa, Śāktās, Devī-sthāna, the Saṁkhya-sages Prakṛti-puruṣa-sthāna. Others call it by other names, such as Hari-hara-sthāna, Śakti-sthāna, Parama-Brahma, Parama-haṁsa, Parama-jyotih, Kula-sthāna, and Parama-Śiva-Ākula. But whatever the name, all speak of the same.

## THE THREE TEMPERAMENTS

The Tantras speak of three temperaments, dispositions, characters (bhāva), or classes of men—namely, the paśu-bhāva (animal), vīra-bhāva (heroic), and divya-bhāva (deva-like or divine). These divisions are based on various modifications of the guṇas (v. *ante*) as they manifest in man (jīva). It has been pointed out[1] that the analogous Gnostic classification of men as material, psychical and spiritual, correspond to the three guṇas of the Sāṁkhya-darśana. In the paśu the rajo-guṇa operates chiefly on tamas, producing such dark characteristics as error (bhrānti), drowsiness (tandrā), and sloth (ālasya). It is however, an error to suppose that the paśu is as such a bad man; on the contrary, a jīva of this class may prove superior to a jīva of the next. If the former, who is greatly bound by matter, lacks enlightenment, the latter may abuse the greater freedom he has won. There are also numerous kinds of paśu, some more some less tāmasik than others. Some there are at the lowest end of the scale, which marks the first advance upon the higher forms of animal life. Others approach and gradually merge into the vīra class. The term paśu comes from the root paś, "to bind". The paśu is, in fact the man who is bound by the bonds (pāśa), of which the Kulārṇava-Tantra enumerates eight—namely, pity (dayā), ignorance and delusion (mohā), fear (bhaya), shame (lajja), disgust

1. Richard Garbe, "Philosophy of Ancient India," p. 48, as also before him, Baur.

(ghṛṇā), family (kula), custom (śīla), and caste (varṇa). Other enumerations are given of the afflictions which, according to some, are sixty-two, but all such larger divisions are merely elaborations of the simpler enumerations. The paśu is also the worldly man, in ignorance and bondage, as opposed to the yogī, and the tattva-jnāni. Three divisions of paśu are also spoken of—namely, sakala, who are bound by the three pāśas, called aṇu (want of knowledge or erroneous knowledge of the self), bheda (the division also induced by māyā of the one self into many), and karma (action and its product). These are the three impurities (mala) called āṇava-mala, māyā-mala, and Karma-mala. Pratayakalā are those bound by the first and last, and Vijnāna-kevala are those bound by āṇava-mala only. He who frees himself of the remaining impurity of aṇu becomes Śiva Himself. The Devī bears the pāśa, and is the cause of them, but She too, is paśupāśa-vimocinī,[1] Liberatrix of the paśu from his bondage.

What has been stated gives the root notion of the term paśu. Men of this class are also described in Tantra by exterior traits, which are manifestations of the interior disposition. So the Kubjika-Tantra[2] says: "Those who belong to paśu-bhāva are simply paśus. A paśu does not touch a yantra, nor make japa of mantra at night. He entertains doubt about sacrifices and Tantra; regards a mantra as being merely letters only.[3] He lacks faith in the guru, and thinks that the image is but a block of stone. He distinguishes one deva from another,[4] and worships without flesh and fish.

---

1. Lalitā-sahasra-nāma (verse 78).

2. Chapter VII.

3. Instead of being Devatā. Similarly the Nityā-Tantrā (see Prāṇatoṣini, 547 et seq).

4. Not recognizing that all are but plural manifestations of the One.

He is always bathing, owing to his ignorance,[1] and talks ill of others.[2] Such an one is called paśu, and he is the worst kind of man."[3] Similarly the Nityā-Tantra[4] describes the paśu as—"He who does not worship at night nor in the evening, nor in the latter part of the day;[5] who avoids sexual intercourse, except on the fifth day after the appearance of the courses[6] (ṛtukālaṁ vinā devi vamanaṁ parivarjayet); who does not eat meat, etc., even on the five auspicious days (pārvana)"; in short, those who, following Vedāchara, Vaiṣṇavācāra, and Śaivācāra, are bound by the Vaidīk rules which govern all paśus.

In the case of vīra-bhāva, rajas more largely works on sattva, yet also largely (though in lessening degrees, until the highest stage of divya-bhāva is reached) works independently towards the production of acts in which sorrow inheres. There are several classes of vīra.

The third, or highest, class of man is he of the divya-bhāva (of which, again, there are several degrees—some but a stage in advance of the highest form of vīra-bhāva, others completely realizing the deva-nature), in which rajas operates on sattva-guṇa to the confirmed preponderance of the latter.

---

1. That is, he only thinks of external and ceremonial purity, not of internal purity of mind, etc.

2. That is, decrying as sectarian-minded Vaiṣṇavas do, all other forms of worship than their own, a common fault of the paśu the world over. In fact, the Picchilā-Tantra (chap. XX) says that the Vaiṣṇava must worship Parameśvara like a paśu.

3. All the Tantras describe the paśu as the lowest form of the three temperaments. Nityā-Tantra, and chap. x of Picchilā Tantra, where paśu-bhāva is described.

4. See Prāṇa-toṣinī, p. 547.

5. As Tantrika vīra do.

6. Taking their usual duration to be four days. This is a Vaidik injunction, as to which see *post*. The Vira and divya are not so bound to maithuna on the fifth day only; that is as to maīthuna as a part of vīrācāra.

The Nityā-Tantra[1] says that of the bhāva the divya is the best, the vīra the next best, and the paśu the lowest; and that devatā-bhāva must be awakened through vīra-bhāva. The Picchilā-Tantra[2] says that the only difference between the vīra and divyā men is that the former are very uddhata, by which is probably meant excitable, through the greater prevalence of the independent working of the rajoguna in them than in the calmer sāttvik temperament. It is obvious that such statements must not be read with legal accuracy. There may be, in fact, a considerable difference between a low type of vīra and the highest type of divya, though it seems to be true that this quality of uddhata which is referred to is the cause of such differences, whether great or small.

The Kubjikā-Tantra[3] describes the marks of the divya as he "who daily does ablutions, saṁdhyā; and wearing clean cloth, the tṛpuṇḍara mark in ashes or red sandal, and ornaments of rudrākṣa-beads, performs japa and arcanā. He gives charity daily also. His faith is strong in Veda, Śāstra, guru, and Deva. He worships the Pitṛi and Deva, performs all the daily rites. He has a great knowledge of mantra. He avoids all food, except that which his guru offers him, and all cruelty and other bad actions, regarding both friend and foe as one and the same. He himself ever speaks the truth, and avoids the company of those who decry the Devatā. He worships thrice daily, and meditates upon his guru daily, and, as a Bhairava, worships Parameśvari with divya-bhāva. All Devās he regards as beneficial.[4] He bows down at the feet of women regarding them as his

1. Loc. cit.

2. Chapter X and so also Utpatti-Tantra (chap. lxiv). See Prāṇatoṣiṇī, p. 570, where also bhāva is described as the dharma of the manas.

3. Chapter VII.

4. He worships all Devas, drawing no distinctions. For instance, an orthodox, up-country Hindu who is a worshipper of Rāma cannot even bear

guru[1] (strīnām pāda-talaṁ dṛṣtvā guru-vad bhāvayet sadā). He worships the Devī at night,[2] and makes japa at night with his mouth full of pan,[3] and makes obeisance to the kula vṛkṣa.[4] He offers everything to the Supreme Devī. He regards this universe as pervaded by strī (śakti), and as Devatā. Śiva is in all men, and the whole brahmāṇḍa is pervaded by Śiva-Śakti. He ever strives for the attainment and maintenance of devatā-bhāva, and is himself of the nature of a Devatā.

Here, again, the Tantra only seeks to give a general picture, the details of which are not applicable to all men of the divya-bhāva class. The passage shows that it, or portions of it, refer to the ritual divya, for some of the practices there referred to would not be performed by the avadhūta, who is above all ritual acts, though he would also share (possibly in intenser degree) the beliefs of divya men of all classes—that he and all else are but manifestations of the universe-pervading Supreme Śakti.

According to the temperament of the sādhaka, so is the form of worship and sādhana. In fact, the specific worship and sādhana of the other classes is strictly prohibited by the Tantra to the paśu.

---

to hear the name of Kṛṣṇa, though both Rāma and Kṛṣṇa are each avatārā of the same Viṣṇu, who is again himself but a partial manifestation of the great Śakti.

1. He is even strī-khanda-paṅkajā-ruhira-bhūṣītah, for he is unaffected by the paśa of ghṛṇā or lajjā.

2. Vaidik worship is by day.

3. That is, after eating, pān being taken after meals.

4. An esoteric term, as to which see Tantrābhidhāna. Similarly (in Nityā-Tantra), he does obeisance to the kulastrī, who is versed in Tantra and mantra, whether she has been brought by a dūtī, is puṁśchāli, or veśyā, and whether youthful or old.

It is said in this Tantra[1] and elsewhere[2] that, in the Kali-yuga, divya and paśu dispositions can scarcely be found. It may be thought difficult at first sight to reconcile this (so far as the paśu is concerned) with other statements as to the nature of these respective classes. The term paśu, in these and similar passages, would appear to be used in a good sense[3] as referring to a man who though tāmasic, yet performs his functions with that obedience to nature which is shown by the still more tāmasic animal creation free from the disturbing influences of rajas, which, if it may be the source of good, may also be, when operating independently, the source of evil.[4]

The Commentator explains the passage cited from the Tantra as meaning that the conditions and character of the Kali-yuga are not such as to be productive of paśu-bhāva (apparently in the sense stated), or to allow of its ācāra (that is, Vaidikācāra). No one, he says, can, fully perform the vedācāra, vaiṣṇavācāra, and śaivācāra rites, without which the Vaidik, Paurānik mantra, and yajña are fruitless. No one now goes through the brahmacārya āśrama, or adopts after the fiftieth year that called vānaprastha. Those whom the Veda does not control cannot expect the fruit of Vaidik observances. On the contrary, men have taken to drink, associate with the low, and are fallen; as are also those men who associate with them. There can therefore be no pure paśu. Under these circumstances the duties prescribed by the Vedas which are appropriate for the

---

1. Chapter I, verse 24.
2. See Śyāmārcana-candrikā, cited in Hara-tattva-didhiti, p. 348.
3. So verse 54 speaks of the paśu as one who should himself procure the leaves, fruits, and water for worship, and not look at a Śūdra, or even think of a woman.
4. For this reason it is possible, in certain cases, that a paśu may attain siddhi through the Tantra quicker than a vīra can.

paśu being incapable of performance, Śiva for the liberation of men of the Kali Age has proclaimed the Āgama. Now, there is no other way." The explanation thus given, therefore, appears to amount to this. The pure type of paśu for whom vedāchāra was designed does not exist. For others who though paśu are not purely so, the Tantra is the governing Śāstra. This however, does not mean that all are now competent for vīrācāra.

It is to be noted, however, that the Prāṇa-toṣinī[1] cites a passage purporting to come from the Mahānirvāṇa-Tantra, which is apparently in direct opposition to the foregoing:

Divya-vīra-mayo bhāvah kalau nāsti kadā-cana.

Kevalaṁ paśu-bhāvena mantra-siddhirbhavenṛṇām.

"In the Kali Age there is no divya or vīrabhāva. It is only by the paśu-bhāva that men may obtain mantra-siddhi."

This matter of the bhāva prevalent in the Kali-yuga has been the subject of considerable discussion and difference of opinion, and is only touched upon here.[2]

1. Pp. 570-571.

2. The subject is a difficult one, and I have given the above-mentioned account with considerable diffidence as to its complete accuracy.

## GURU AND ŚIṢYA

THE Guru is the religious teacher and spiritual guide to whose direction orthodox Hindus of all divisions of worshippers submit themselves. There is in reality but one Guru. The ordinary human Guru is but the manifestation on the phenomenal plane of the Ādi-nāthā Mahā-kāla, the Supreme Guru abiding in Kailāsa.[1] He it is who enters into and speaks with the voice of the earthly Guru at the time of giving mantra.[2] Guru is the root (mūla) of dīkṣā (initiation). Dīkṣā is the root of mantra. Mantra is the root of Devatā; and Devatā is the root of siddhi. The Munda-mālā-Tantra says that mantra is born of Guru and Devatā of mantra, so that the Guru occupies the position of a grandfather to the Iṣta-devatā.

It is the Guru who initiates and helps, and the relationship between him and the disciple (śiṣya) continues until the attainment of monistic siddhi. Manu says: "Of him who gives natural birth and of him who gives knowledge of the Veda, the giver of sacred knowledge is the more venerable father. Since second or divine birth insures life to the twice-born in this world and the next." The Śāstra is, indeed, full of the greatness of Guru.[3] The guru is not

---

1. Guru sthānaṁ hi kailāsaṁ (Yoginī-Tantra, chap. i).

2. Mantra-pradāna-kāle hi mānuṣe nāga-nandini,
Adhiṣthānaṁ bhavet tatra mahākālasya śaṁkari,
Atastu gurutā devī mānuṣe nātra saṁśayah (ibid).

3. See chap. i of the Tantra-sāra, which also deals with the qualities of the Guru; the relationship between him and the disciple, qualities of the disciple and so forth.

to be thought of as a mere man. There is no difference between Guru, mantra, and Deva. Guru is father, mother, and Brahman. Guru, it is said, can save from the wrath of Śiva but none can save from the wrath of the Guru. Attached to this greatness there is, however, responsibility; for the sins of the disciple recoil upon him.

Three lines of Gurus are worshipped; heavenly (divyānga), siddha (siddhānga), and human (mānavānga).[1] The Kula-gurus are four in number, viz.: the Guru, Parama-guru, Parāpara-guru, Parameṣṭi-guru; each of these being the guru of the preceding one. According to the Tantra, a woman with the necessary qualifications may be a guru, and give initiation.[2] Good qualities are required in the disciple,[3] and according to the Sāra-saṁgraha a guru should examine and test the intending disciple for a year.[4] The qualifications of a good disciple are stated to be good birth, purity of soul (śuddhātmā), and capacity for enjoyment, combined with desire for liberation (puruṣārtha-parāyaṇah).[5] Those who are lewd (kāmuka), adulterous (paradārātura), constantly addicted to sin (sadā pāpa-kriya), ignorant, slothful and devoid of religion, should be rejected.[6]

The perfect sādhaka who is entitled to the knowledge of all Śāstras is he who is pure-minded, whose senses are controlled (jitendriyah), who is ever engaged in doing good to all beings, free from false notions of dualism, attached to the speaking of, taking shelter with and living

1. See Chapter VI, "The Great Liberation."

2. See *post.*

3. Tantra sāra (chap. i).

4. See Tantrasāra (chap. i) and Prāṇa-toṣinī, p. 108, Matsya-sūkta Mahātantra, (chap. xiii).

5. Matsya-sūkta Tantra (chap. xiii), Prāṇa-toṣinī, 108.

6. Mahārudrā-yāmala, 1. Khanda (chap. xv), 2. Khanda (chap. ii).

in the supreme unity of the Brahman.[1] So long as Śakti is not fully communicated (see next page) to the śiṣya's body from that of the guru, so long the conventional relation of guru and śiṣya exists. A man is śiṣya only so long as he is sādhaka. When, however, siddhi is attained, both Guru and Śiṣya are above this dualism. With the attainment of pure monism, naturally this relation, as all others, disappears.

1. Gandharva-Tantra (chap. ii).

## INITIATION : DĪKṢĀ

INITIĀTION[1] is the giving of mantra by the guru. At the time of initiation the guru must first establish the life of the guru in his own body; that is the vital force (prāṇa-śakti) of the Supreme Guru whose abode is in the thousand-petalled lotus. As an image is the instrument (yantra) in which divinity (devatva) inheres, so also is the body of guru. The day prior thereto the guru should, according to Tantra, seat the intending candidate on a mat of kuśa-grass. He then makes japa of a "sleep mantra" (supta-mantra) in his ear, and ties his crown lock. The disciple, who should have fasted and observed sexual continence repeats the mantra thrice, prostrates himself at the feet of the guru, and then retires to rest. Initiation, which follows, gives spiritual knowledge and destroys sin. As one lamp is lit at the flame of another, so the divine śakti, consisting of mantra, is communicated from the guru's body to that of the Śiṣya. Without dīkṣā, japa of the mantra, pūjā, and other ritual acts, are said to be useless. Certain mantras are also said to be forbidden to śūdras and women. A note, however, in the first Chalākṣara-Sūtrā to the Lalitā[2] would, however, show that even the śudras are not debarred the

---

1. As to who may initiate see Tantrasāra, chap. i.

2. First Chalākṣara-Sūtra. This is an index to the Sahasra-nāmā, like the Sarvānukramaṇikā to the Veda. There are three svaras in laukika-vyākaraṇa—viz, udātta, the high accent, anudātta, its opposite or the low accent and, svaritā, which Pāṇini says is the combination (samāhṛta) of both. Pracaya is Vaidīk (chāndasa).

use even of the Praṇava, as is generally asserted. For according to the Kālikā-Purāna (when dealing with svara or tone), whilst the udātta, anudātta, and pracaya are appropriate to the first of these castes, the svara, called aukāra, with anusvara and nāda, is appropriate to śudra, who may use the Praṇava, either at the begining or end of mantra, but not, as the dvija may, at both places. The mantra chosen for initiation should.be suitable (anukūla). Whether a mantra is sva-kūla or a-kūla to the person about to be initiated is ascertained by the kula-cakra, the zodiacal circle called rāśicakra and other cakra which may be found described in the Tantrasāra. Initiation by a woman is efficacious; that by a mother is eight-fold so.[1] Certain special forms of initiation, called abhiṣeka, are described in the next note.

1. Tantrasāra, loc cit.

# ABHIṢEKA

Abhiseka[1] is of eight kinds, and the forms of abhiṣeka which follow the first at later stages, mark greater and greater degrees of initiation. The first śāktābhiṣeka is given on entrance into the path of sādhana. It is so called because the guru then reveals to the śiṣya the preliminary mysteries of śakti-tattva. By it the śiṣya is cleansed of all sinful or evil śakti or proclivities, and acquires a wonderful new śakti.[2] The next, pūrnābhiṣeka is given in the stage beyond dakṣinācāra, when the disciple has qualified himself by puraścaraṇa and other practices to receive it. Here the real work of sādhana begins. Āsana, yama, etc., strengthen the disciple's determination (pratijnā) to persevere along the higher stages of sādhana. The third is the difficult stage commenced by krama-dīkṣābhiṣeka, in which it is said the great Vaśiṣṭha became involved, and in which the Ṛṣi Viśvāmitra acquired brahmajñānā and so became a Brāhmana. The sacred thread is now worn round the neck like a garland. The śiṣya, then undergoing various ordeals (parīkṣā), receives sāmrājyābhiṣeka and mahāsāmrājyābhiṣeka, and at length arrives at the most difficult of all stages introduced by yoga-dīkṣābhiṣeka. In the previous stages the sādhaka has performed the pañcāṅga-puraścaraṇa, and, with the

---

1. Sprinkling, anointing, inaugurating, consecration as of a king or disciple.

2. Of the śāktābhiṣeka two forms are also mentioned—rājā and yogi (see Prāṇatoṣinī, 254; Vāmakeśvara Tantrā, chap. 1; Niruttara-Tantra, (chap. vii). As to what follows, see Tantrarahasya, cited *post*.

assistance of his guru (with whom he must constantly reside, and whose instructions he must receive direct), he does the pañcāṅga-yoga—that is, the last five limbs of the aṣṭānga. He is thereafter qualified for pūrnadīkṣābhiṣeka, and, following that, mahā-pūrṇa-dīkṣābhiṣekā, sometimes called virāja-grahaṇābhiṣeka. On the attainment of perfection in this last grade, the sādhaka performs his own funeral rites (śrāddha), makes pūrnāhuti with his sacred thread and crown lock. The relation of guru and śiṣya now ceases. From this point he ascends by himself until he realizes the great saying, So'ham ("I am He"). At this stage, which the Tantra calls jīvan-mukta (liberated whilst yet living) he is called parama-haṁsa.

# SĀDHANA

Sādhana is that which produces siddhi (*q.v.*). It is the means, or practice, by which the desired end may be attained, and consists in the exercise and training of the body and psychic faculties, upon the gradual perfection of which siddhi follows; the nature and degree of which, again, depends upon the progress made towards the realization of the ātmā, whose veiling vesture the body is. The means employed are various, such as worship (pūjā), exterior or mental; śāstric learning; austerities (tapas); the panca-tattva, mantra, and so forth. Sādhana takes on a special character, according to the end sought. Thus, sādhana for brahma-jñāna, which consists in the acquisition of internal control (śama) over buddhi, manas, and ahaṁkāra; external control (dama) over the ten indriyas, discrimination between the transitory and the external, and renunciation both of the world and heaven (svarga), is obviously different from that prescribed for, say, the purposes of the lower magic. The sādhaka and sādhika are respectively the man and woman who perform sādhana. They are, according to their physical, mental, and moral qualities, divided into four classes—mṛdu, madhya, adhimātraka, and the highest adhimātrama, who is qualified (adhikārī) for all forms of yoga. In a similar way the Kaula division of worshippers are divided into the prakṛti, or common Kaula following vīrācārā, addicted to ritual practice, and sādhana, with pañca-tattva; the madhyamakaulika, or middling Kaula, accomplishing the same sādhana, but with a mind more turned towards meditation, knowledge, and samādhi; and the highest type of Kaula (kaulikottama), who, having surpassed all ritualism meditates upon the Universal Self.

## WORSHIP

THERE are four different forms of worship corresponding with four states (bhāva).[1] The realization that the jīvātma and paramātma are one, that everything is Brahman, and that nothing but the Brahman exists, is the highest state or brahma-bhāva. Constant meditation by the yoga process upon the Devata in the heart is the lower and middlemost (dhyāna-bhāva), japa (*q.v.*) and stava (hymns and prayer) is still lower, and the lowest of all is mere external worship (pūjā) (*q.v.*). Pūjā-bhāva is that which arises out of the dualistic notions of worshipper and worshipped; the servant and the Lord. This dualism exists in greater or less degree in all states except the highest. But for him who, having realized the advaita-tattva, knows that all is Brahman, there is neither worshipper nor worshipped, neither yoga nor pūjā, nor dhāraṇa, dhyāna, stava, japa, vrata, or other ritual or process of sādhana.

In external worship there is worship either of an image (pratimā), or of a yantra (*q.v.*), which takes its place. The sādhaka should first worship inwardly the mental image of the form assumed by the Devī, and then by the life-giving (prāṇa-pratiṣṭhā) ceremony infuse the image with Her life by the communication to it of the light and energy (tejas) of the Brahman which is within him to the image without, from which there bursts the lustre of Her whose substance is consciousness itself (caitanya-mayī). She

---

1. See "Principles of Tantra," 2nd Edition, p. 1084.

exists as Śakti in stone or metal, or elsewhere, but is there veiled and seemingly inert. Caitanya (consciousness) is aroused by the worshipper through the prāṇa-pratiṣthā mantra.

Rites (karma) are of two kinds. Karma is either nitya or naimittika. The first is both daily and obligatory, and is done because so ordained. Such are the sandhyā (*v. post*), which in the case of Śūdras is in the Tāntrik form; and daily pūjā (*v. post*) of the Iṣta- and Kula-Devatā (*v. post*); and for Brāhmaṇas the panca-mahā-yajna (*v. post*). The second or conditional karma is occasional and voluntary, and is kāmya when done to gain some particular end, such as yajña for a particular object; tapas with the same end (for certain forms of tapas are also nitya); and vrata (*v. post*).

The Śūdra is precluded from the performance of Vaidik rites, or the reading of Vedas, or the recital of the Vaidik mantra. His worship is practically limited to that of the Iṣta-Devatā and the Bāṇa-linga-pūja, with Tāntrik and Paurāṇik mantra and such vratas as consist in penance and charity. In other cases the vrata is performed through a Brāhmaṇa. The Tantra makes no caste distinctions as regards worship. All may read the Tantras, perform the Tāntrik worship, such as the sandhyā (*v. post*), and recite the Tāntrik mantra, such as the Tāntrik Gāyatri. All castes, and even the lowest caṇḍāḷa, may be a member of a cakra, or Tāntrik circle of worship. In the cakra all its members partake of food and drink together and are deemed to be greater than Brāhmaṇas; though upon the break-up of the cakra the ordinary caste and social relations are re-established. All are competent for the special Tāntrik worship, for, in the words of the Gautamīya-Tantra, the Tantra-Śāstra is for all castes and for all women.[1] The latter are

1. Sarva-varnādhikārasyeha nārīnām yogya eva ca (chap. i).

also excluded under the present Vaidik system, though it is said by Śankha Dharma-śāstra-kāra that the wife may, with the consent of her husband, fast, take vows, perform homa and vratā,[1] etc. According to the Tantra, a woman may not only receive mantra, but may, as a Guru, initiate and give it.[2] She is worshipful as Guru, and as wife of Guru.[3] The Devī is Herself Guru of all Śāstras[4] and women, as, indeed, all females who are Her embodiments are, in a peculiar sense, Her earthly representatives.

## FORMS OF ĀCĀRA

There are seven, or, as some say, nine, divisions of worshippers. The extra divisions are bracketed in the following quotation. The Kulārṇava-Tantra mentions seven, which are given in their order of superiority, the first being the lowest: Vedācāra, Vaiṣṇavācāra, Śaivācāra, Dakṣiṇācārā, Vāmācāra, Siddhāntācāra, (Aghorācāra,[5] Yogācāra), and Kaulācāra, the highest of all.[6] The ācāra is the way, custom and practice of a particular class of sādhakas. They

---

1. It has been said that neither a virgin (kumārī), a pregnant woman (garbhiṇī), nor a woman during her period, can perform vṛata.

2. Rudra-yāmala, 2 Khaṇda (chap. ii); 1 Khaṇda (chap. xv.), where the qualifications are stated.

3. Ibid., 1 Khaṇda (chap. i); Mātrkā-bheda-Tantra (chap. viii); Annadākalpa Tantra cited in Prāṇa-toṣiṇī, p. 68. As the Yoginī-Tantra says, gurupatnī maheśāni gūrureva (ch. p. i).

4. Kaṅkāla-mālinī-Tantra (chap. ii).

5. This is generally regarded as a distinct sect though the author below cited says it is, in fact, not so. Aghora means, it is said, one who is liberated from the terrible (ghora) saṁsāra, but in any case, many worshippers for want of instruction by a siddha-guru have degenerated into mere eaters of corpses.

6. Chapter II. A short description (of little aid) is given in the Visvasāra-Tantra (chap. xxiv). See also Hara-tattva-dīdhiti, fourth edition, pp. 339, et seq.

are not, as sometimes supposed, different sects, but stages through which the worshipper in this or other births has to pass before he reaches the supreme stage of the Kaula. Vedācāra, which consists in the daily practice of the Vaidik rites, is the gross body (sthūla-deha), which comprises within it all other ācāras, which are, as it were, its subtle bodies (sūkṣma-deha) of various degrees. The worship is largely of an external and ritual character, the object of which is to strengthen dharma. This is the path of action (kriyā-mārga). In the second stage the worshipper passes from blind faith to an understanding of the supreme protecting energy of the Brahman, towards which he has the feelings of devotion. This is the path of devotion (bhakti-mārga), and the aim at this stage is the union of it and faith previously acquired. With an increasing determination to protect dharma and destroy adharma, the sādhaka passes into Śaivācāra, the warrior (kṣatriya) stage, wherein to love and mercy are added strenuous striving and the cultivation of power. There is union of faith, devotion (bhakti), and inward determination (antar-lakṣa). Entrance is made upon the path of knowledge (jñāna-mārga). Following this is Dakṣinācāra, which in Tantra does not mean "right-hand worship", but "favourable" — that is, that ācāra which is favourable to the accomplishment of the higher sādhana, and whereof the Devī is the Dakṣiṇā-Kālikā. This stage commences when the worshipper can make dhyāna and dhāraṇā of the threefold śakti of the Brahman (kriyā, icchā, jñāna), and understands the mutual connection (samanvaya) of the three gunas until he receives purṇābhiṣekā (*q.v.*). At this stage the sādhaka

1. See as to this and following the Sanātana-sādhana-tattva, or Tantra-rahasya of Sacchidānanda Svāmi.

is Śakta, and qualified for the worship of the threefold śakti of Brahmā, Viṣṇu, Maheśvara. He is fully initiated in the Gāyatri-mantra, and worships the Devī Gāyatri, the Dakṣiṇā-Kālikā, or Ādyā Śakti—the union of the three Śaktis. This is the stage of individualistic Brāhmanattva, and its aim is the union of faith, devotion, and determination, with a knowledge of the threefold energies. After this a change of great importance occurs, marking, as it does, the entry upon the path of return (nivṛtti). This it is which has led some to divide the ācāra into the two broad divisions of Dakṣiṇācāra (including the first four) and Vāmācāra, (inluding the last three), it being said that men are born into Dakṣiṇācāra, but are received by initiation into Vāmācāra. The latter term does not mean, as is vulgarly supposed, "left-hand worship" but worship in which woman (vāmā) enters, that is latā-sādhana. In this ācāra there is also worship of the Vāmā-Devī. Vāmā is here "adverse," in that the stage is adverse to pravṛtti, which governed in varying degrees the preceding ācāra, and entry is here made upon the path of nivṛtti, or return to the source whence the world sprung. Up to the fourth stage the sādhaka followed pravṛttimārga, the outgoing path which led from the source, the path of worldly enjoyment, albeit curbed by dharma. At first unconsciously, and later consciously, sādhana sought to induce nivṛtti, which, however, can only fully appear after the exhaustion of the forces of the outward current. In Vāmācāra, however, the sādhaka commences to directly destroy pravṛtti, and with the help of the Guru (whose help throughout is in this necessary)[1] to cultivate nivṛtti. The method at this stage is to use the force of pravṛtti in

---

1. It is comparatively easy to lay down rules for the pravṛtti-mārga, but nothing can be achieved in Vāmācāra without the Guru's help.

such a way as to render them self-destructive. The passions which bind may be so employed as to act as forces whereby particular life of which they are the strongest manifestation is raised to the universal life. Passion, which has hitherto run downwards and outwards to waste, is directed inwards and upwards, and transformed to power. But it is not only the lower physical desires of eating, drinking, and sexual intercourse which must be subjugated. The sādhaka must at this stage commence to cut off all the eight bonds (pāśa) which mark the paśu which the Kūlārṇava-Tantra enumerātes as pity (dayā), ignorance (moha), shame (lajjā), family (kula), custom (śila), and caste (varṇa).[1] When Śrī-Kṛṣṇa stole the clothes of the bathing Gopīs, and made them approach him naked, he removed the artificial coverings which are imposed on man in the saṁsārā. The Gopīs were eight, as are the bonds (pāśa), and the errors by which the jīva is misled are the clothes which Śrī Kṛṣṇa stole. Freed of these, the jīva is liberated from all bonds arising from his desires, family, and society. He then reaches the stage of Śiva (śivatva). It is the aim of Vāmācāra to liberate from the bonds which bind men to the saṁsāra, and to qualify the sādhaka for the highest grades of sādhana in which the sāttvika guna predominates. To the truly sāttvik there is neither attachment nor fear nor disgust. That which has been commenced in these stages is by degrees completed in those which follow—viz.: Siddhāntācāra, and according to some, Aghorācāra and Yogācārā. The sādḥaka becomes more and more freed from the darkness of the saṁsāra, and is attached to nothing, hates nothing, and is ashamed of nothing, having freed himself of the

---

1. There are various enumerations of the "afflictions" (pāśa) which are, however merely elaborations of the smaller divisions. Thus, according to the Devi-Bhāgavata, Moha is ignorance or bewilderment, and Maha-moha is desire of worldly pleasures.

artificial bonds of family, caste, and society. The sādhaka becomes, like, Śiva himself, a dweller in the cremation ground (smaśāna). He learns to reach the upper heights of sādhana and the mysteries of yoga. He learns the movements of the different vāyus in the microcosm, the kṣudra-brahmānda, the regulation of which controls the inclinations and propensities (vritti). He learns also the truths which concern the măcrocosm (brahmāṇḍa). Here also the Guru teaches him the inner core of Vedācāra. Initiation by yoga-dikṣā fully qualifies him for yogācāra. On attainment of perfection in aṣṭāṅga-yoga, he is fit to enter the higest stage of Kaulācāra.

Kaula-dharma is in no wise sectarian, but, on the contrary, is the heart of all sects. This is the true meaning of the phrase which, like many another touching the Tantra, is misunderstood, and used to fix the kaula with hypocrisy—antah-śāktāh, bahih-śaivāh, subhāyāṁ vaiṣṇavāmatāh, nānā-rūpadharah kaulāh vicaranti mahītāle; (outwardly Śaivas; in gatherings,[1] Vaiṣṇavas; at heart, Sāktas; under various forms the Kaūlas wander on earth). A Kaula is one who has passed through these and other stages, which have as their own inmost doctrine (whether these worshippers know it or not) that of Kaulācāra. It is indifferent what the Kaūla's apparent sect may be. The form is nothing and everything. It is nothing in the sense that it has no power to narrow the Kaula's own inner life; it is everything in the sense that knowledge may infuse its apparent limitations with an universal meaning. So understood, form is never a bond. The Visva-sāra Tantra says[2] of the Kaula that "for him there is neither rule of time nor place. His actions are unaffected either by the phases of

1. The vaiṣṇavas are wont to gather together for worship singing the praise of Hari, etc.

2. Chapter XXIV.

the moon or the position of the stars. The Kaula roams the earth in differing forms. At times adhering to social rules (śiṣta), he at others appears, according to their standard, to be fallen (bhraṣta). At times, again, he seems to be as unearthly as a ghost (bhūta or piśāca). To him no difference is there between mud and sandal paste, his son and an enemy, home and the cremation ground."

At this stage the sādhaka attains to Brahma-jñāna, which is the true gnosis in its perfect form. On receiving mahāpūrṇa-dīkṣā he performs his own funeral rites and is dead to the saṁsāra. Seated alone in some quiet place, he remains in constant samādhi, and attains its nirvikalpa form. The great Mother, the Supreme Prakṛti Mahāśakti, dwells in the heart of the sādhaka, which is now the cremation ground wherein all passions have been burnt away. He becomes a Parama-haṁsa, who is liberated whilst yet living (jīvan-mukta).

It must not, however, be supposed that each of these stages must necessarily be passed through by each jīva in a single life. On the contrary, they are ordinarily traversed in the course of a multitude of births. The weaving of the spiritual garment is recommenced where, in a previous birth, it was dropped on death. In the present life a sādhaka may commence at any stage. If he is born into Kaulācāra, and so is a Kaula in its fullest sense, it is because in previous births he has by sādhana, in the preliminary stages, won his entrance into it. Knowledge of Śakti is, as the Niruttara-Tantra says, acquired after many births; and, according to the Mahānirvāṇa-Tantra, it is by merit acquired in previous births that the mind is inclined to Kaulācāra.

## MANTRA

Śabda, or sound, which is of the Brahman, and as such the cause of the Brahmaṇḍa, is the manifestation of the Cit-śakti itself. The Viśva-sāra-Tantra says[1] that the Para-brahman, as Śabda-brahman, whose substance is all mantra, exists in the body of the jīvātmā. It is either unlettered (dhvani) or lettered (varṇa). The former, which produces the latter, is the subtle aspect of the jīva's vital śakti. As the Prapañca-sāra states, the brahmāṇḍa is pervaded by śakti, consisting of dhvani, also called nāda, prāṇa, and the like. The manifestation of the gross form (sthūla) of śabda is not possible unless śabda exists in a subtle (sūkṣma) form. Mantras are all aspects of the Brahman and manifestations of Kulakuṇḍalinī Philosophically śabda is the guna of ākāśa, or ethereal space. It is not, however, produced by ākāśa, but manifests in it. Śabda is itself the Brahman. In the same way, however, as in outer space, waves of sound are produced by movements of air (vāyu); so in the space within the jīva's body waves of sound are produced according to the movements of the vital air (prāṇa-vāyu) and the process of inhalation and exhalation. Śabda first appears at the mūlādhāra, and that which is known to us as such is, in fact, the śakti which gives life to the jīva. She it is who, in the mūlādhāra, is the cause of the sweet indistinct and murmuring dhvani, which sounds like the humming of a black bee.

The extremely subtle aspect of sound which first appears in the Mūlādhārā is called parā; less subtle when it has reached the heart, it is known as paśyanti. When connected with buddhi it becomes more gross, and is called madhyamā. Lastly, in its fully gross form, it issues from the mouth as vaikharī. As Kula-kuṇḍalinī, whose substance is all varṇa and dhvani is but the manifestation of, and Herself the Paramātmā; so the substance

---

1. Chapter II.

of all mantra is cit, notwithstanding their external manifestation, as sound, letters, or words; in fact, the letters of the alphabet, which are known as akṣara, are nothing but the yantra of the akṣara, or imperishable Brahman. This, however, is only realized by the sādhaka when his śakti, generated by sādhana, is united with the mantra-śakti.

It is the sthūla or gross form of Kulakuṇḍalini, appearing in different aspects as different Devatās, which is the presiding Devatā (adhiṣthātrī) of all mantra, though it is the subtle or sūkṣma form at which all sādhakas aim. When the mantraśakti is awakened by the sādhana the presiding Devatā appears, and when perfect mantra-siddhi is acquired, the Devatā, who is saccidānanda, is revealed. The relations of varṇa, nāda, bindu, vowel and consonant in a mantra, indicate the appearance of Devatā in different forms. Certain vibhūtis, or aspects, of the Devata are inherent in certain varṇas, but perfect Śakti does not appear in any but a whole mantra. Any word or letter of the mantra cannot be a mantra. Only that mantra in which the playful Devatā has revealed any of Her particular aspects can reveal that aspect, and is therefore called the individual mantra of that one of Her particular aspects. The form of a particular Devatā, therefore, appears out of the particular mantra of which that Devatā, is the adhiṣthātrī-Devatā.

A mantra is composed of certain letters arranged in definite sequence of sounds of which the letters are the representative signs. To produce the designed effect mantra must be intoned in the proper way, according to svara (rhythm), and varṇa (sound).[1] Their textual source is to

---

1. For those reasons a mantra, when translated, ceases to be such, and becomes a mere sentence.

be found in Veda, Purāṇa, and Tantra. The latter is essentially the mantra-śāstra, and so it is said of the embodied śāstra, that Tantra, which consists of mantra, is the paramātmā, the Vedas are the jīvātmā, Darśana (systems of philosophy) are the senses, Purāṇas are the body, and Smṛtis are the limbs. Tantra is thus the śakti of consciousness, consisting of mantra. A mantra is not the same thing as prayer or self-dedication (ātma-nivedana). Prayer is conveyed in what words the worshipper chooses, and bears its meaning on its face. It is only ignorance of śāstrik principles which supposes that mantra is merely the name for the words in which one expresses what one has to say to the Divinity. If it were, the sādhaka might choose his own language without recourse to the eternal and determined sounds of Śāstra.

A mantra may, or may not, convey on its face its meaning. Bīja (seed) mantra, such as Aiṁ, Klīṁ, Hrīṁ, have no meaning, according to the ordinary use of language. The initiate, however, knows that their meaning is the own form (sva-rūpa) of the particular Devatā, whose mantra they are, and that they are the dhvani which makes all letters sound and which exists in all which we say or hear. Every mantra is, then, a form (rūpa) of the Brahman. Though, therefore, manifesting in the form and sound of the letters of the alphabet, Śāstra says that they go to Hell who think that the Guru is but a stone, and the mantra but letters of the alphabet.

From manana, or thinking, arises the real understanding of the monistic truth, that the substance of the Brahman and the brahmāṇḍa are one and the same. Man- of mantra comes from the first syllable of manana, and -tra from trāṇa, or liberation from the bondage of the saṁsāra or phenomenal world. By the combination of man- and -tra, that is called mantra which calls forth (āmantraṇa), the catur-varga (*vide post*), or four aims of sentient being.[1] Whilst, therefore, mere prayer often ends in nothing but physical sound, mantra is a potent compelling force, a word of power (the fruit of which is mantra-siddhi), and is thus effective to produce caturvarga, advaitic perception, and mukti. Thus it is said that siddhi is the certain result of japa (*q.v.*).

By Mantra the sought for (sādhya) Devata is attained and compelled. By siddhi in mantra is opened the vision of the three worlds. Though the purpose of worship (pūjā), reading (pātha), hymn (stava), sacrifice (homa), dhyāna, dhāraṇā, and samādhi (*vide post*), and that of the dīkṣā-mantra are the same, yet the latter is far more powerful, and this for the reason that, in the first, the sādhakā's sādhana-śakti only operates, whilst in the case of mantra that sādhana-śakti works, in conjunction with mantra-śakti which has the revelation and force of fire, and than which nothing is more powerful. The special mantra which is received at initiation (dīkṣā) is the bīja or seed mantra, sown in the field of the sādhaka's heart, and the Tāntrik saṁdhyā, nyāsa, pūja and the like are the stem and branches upon which hymns of praise (stuti) and prayer and homage (vandana) are the leaves and flower, and the kavaca, consisting of mantra, the fruit.

Mantras are solar (saura) and lunar (saumya), and are masculine, feminine, or neuter. The solar are masculine and lunar feminine. The masculine and neuter forms are called mantra. The feminine mantra is known as vidyā. The neuter mantra, such as the Paurānik-mantra, ending with namah, are said to lack the force and vitality of the others. The masculine and feminine mantras end differently.

---

1. See "Garland of Letters" and chapter on Mantra-tattva in "The Principles of Tantra".

Thus, Huṁ, Phat, are masculine terminations, and "thaṁ", svāhā, are feminine ones.[1]

The Nityā-Tantra gives various names to mantra, according to the number of their syllables, a one-syllabled mantra being called piṇḍa, a three-syllabled one kartarī, a mantra with four to nine syllables bīja, with ten to twenty syllables mantra, and mantra with more than twenty syllables mālā. Commonly, however, the term bīja is applied to monosyllabic mantra. The Tāntrik mantras called bīja (seed) are so named because they are the seed of the fruit, which is siddhi, and because they are the very quintessence of mantra. They are short, unetymological vocables, such as Hrīṁ, Śrīṁ, Krīṁ, Aiṁ, Phat, etc., which will be found throughout the text.[2] Each Devatā has His or Her bīja.[3] The primary mantra of a Devatā is known as the root mantra (mūla-mantra). It is also said that the word mūla denotes the subtle body of the Devatā called Kāma-kalā. The utterance of a mantra without knowledge of its meaning or of the mantra method is a mere movement of the lips and nothing more. The mantra sleeps. There are various processes preliminary to, and involved in, its right utterance, which processes again consist of mantra, such as, for purification of the mouth (mukha-śodhana),[4] purification of the tongue (jihva-śodhana)[5] and

1. See Sāradā-tilaka (chap. ii); Nārada-pānca-rātra (chap. vii), the Prayogasāra and Prāṇa-toṣinī, (p. 70). If it be asked why formless things of mind are given sex, the answer is for the sake of the requirements of the worshipper.

2. See also the mantra portion of the Atharva-Veda to which the Tantra stands in close relation.

3. Krīṁ (Kālī), Hrīṁ (Māyā), Raṁ (Agnī), Eṁ (Yoni), etc.

4. See Chapter X, Sāradā-Tilaka, Japa of praṇava or the mantra varies with the Devatā—e.g., Oṁ Hsau for Bhairava.

5. Seven japas of one-lettered bīja triplicated, praṇava triplicated, then one-lettered bīja triplicated.

of the mantra (aśauca-bhaṅga),[1] kulluka,[2] nirvāna,[3] setu,[4] nidhrā-bhanga, awakening of mantra,[5] mantra-caitanya, or giving of life or vitality to the mantra.[6] Mantrārthabhāvana, forming of mental image of the Divinity.[7] There are also ten saṁskāras of the mantra.[8] Dīpanī is seven japas of the bīja, preceded and followed by oṁ. Where hrīṁ is employed instead of Oṁ it is prāṇa-yoga. Yoni-mudrā is meditation on the Guru in the head and on the Iṣta-devatā in the heart, and then on the Yoni-rūpā Bhagavati from the head to the mūlādhāra, and from the mūlādhāra to the head, making japa of the yoni bīja (eṁ) ten times.[9] The mantra itself is Devatā. The worshipper awakens and vitalizes it by cit-śakti, putting away all thought of the letter, piercing the six Cakras, and contemplating the spotless One.[10] The śakti of the mantra is the vācaka-śakti, or the means by which the vācya-śakti or object of the mantra is attained. The mantra lives by the energy of the former. The saguṇā-śakti is awakened

---

1. Japa of mūla-mantra preceded and followed by praṇava. As to the 'birth" and "death" defilements of a mantra, see Tantrasāra 75, *et seq.*

2. See Sāradā (loc. cit.). Thus Kulluka (which is done over the head) of Kūlikā is Māyā (see Puraścaraṇa-Bodhinī, p. 48, and Tantrasāra).

3. Japa of Mūla- and Mātṛkā-bījā in the Maṇipūra.

4. Generally the mahāmantra Oṁ or Māyā-bījā Hrīṁ, but also varies. Thus Setu of Kāli is her own bījā (krīṁ), of Tārā, Kuraca, etc.

5. Japa of the Mantra in preceded and followed by *īṁ* seven times.

6. Jaya of Mūla-mantra in Maṇipūra preceded and followed by Mātṛkā-bīja. Meditating on the mūla-mantra in the sahāsrāra, anāhata, mūlā-dhāra, with Hūṁ, and again in Sahasrāra. The mūla is the principal mantra, such as the pancadaśi.

7. Lit., thinking of meaning of mantra or thinking of the mātṛkā in the mantra which constitute the Devatā from foot to head.

8. See Tantrasāra, p. 90.

9. See Purohita-darpaṇam.

10. Kubjikā-Tantra (chap. v).

by sādhana and worshipped, and she it is who opens the portals whereby the vācya-śakti is reached. Thus the Mother in Her saguṇa form is the presiding deity (adhiṣthātrī-Devatā) of the Gāyatrī-mantra. As the nirguṇa (formless) One, She is its vācya-śakti. Both are in reality one and the same; but the jīva, by the laws of his nature and its three guṇas, must first meditate on the gross (sthūla) form[1] before he can realize the subtle (sūkṣma) form, which is his liberator.

The mantra of a Devatā is the Devatā. The rhythmical vibrations of its sounds not merely regulate the unsteady vibrations of the sheaths of the worshipper, thus transforming him, but from it arises the form of the Devatā which it is.[2] Mantra-siddhi is the ability to make a mantra efficacious and to gather its fruit[3] in which case the mantra is called mantra-siddha. Mantras are classified as siddha, sādhya, susiddha, and ari, according as they are friends, servers, supporters, or destroyers—a matter which is determined for each sādhaka by means of cakra calculations.

## THE GĀYATRĪ-MANTRA

The Gāyatrī is the most sacred of all Vaidik mantras. In it the Veda lies embodied as in its seed. It runs: Oṁ

---

1. These forms are not merely the creatures of the imagination of the worshipper, as some "modernist" Hindus suppose, but, according to orthodox notions, the forms in which the Deity, in fact, appears to the worshipper.

2. Śṛnu devī pravakṣyāmi bījānām deva-rūpatāṁ.
Mantroccāraṇamātreṇa, deva-rūpaṁ prajāyate.
—(Bṛhad-gandharva-Tantra, chap. v.)

3. Yaṁ Yaṁ prārthayate kāmaṁ
Taṁ tamāpnoti niścitam.
(Whatever the sādhaka desires that he surely obtains)
—Prāṇa-toṣinī, 619.

bhūr-bhuvah-svah: tat savitur vareṇyam bhargo devaśya dhīmahi dhiyo yo nah pracodayāt. Oṁ. "Let us contemplate the wondrous spirit of the Divine Creator (Savitṛ) of the earthly, atmospheric, and celestial spheres. May He direct our minds, that is, 'towards' the attainment of dharma, artha, kāma, and mokṣa, Oṁ."

The Gāyatrī-Vyākaraṇa of Yoga-Yājnavalkya thus explains the following words: Tat, that.[1] The word yat (which) is understood.[2] Savituh is the possessive case of Savitṛ derived from the root sū, "to bring forth." Savitṛ is, therefore, the Bringer-forth of all that exists. The Sun (Sūrya) is the cause of all that exists, and of the state in which they exist. Bringing forth and creating all things, it is called Savitṛ. The Bhaviṣya-Purāṇa says Sūrya is the visible Devatā. He is the Eye of the world and the Maker of the day. There is no other Devatā eternal like unto Him. This universe has emanated from and will be again absorbed into, Him. Time is of and in Him. The planets, stars, the Vasus, Rudras, Vāyu, Agni, and the rest are but parts of Him. By Bhargah is meant the Āditya-devatā, dwelling in the region of the Sun (sūrya-maṇḍala) in all His might and glory. He is to the Sun what our spirit (ātmā) is to our body. Though He is in the region of the sun in the outer or material sphere He also dwells in our inner selves. He is the light of the light in the solar circle, and is the light of the lives of all beings. As He is in the outer ether, so also is He in the ethereal region of the heart. In the outer ether He is Sūrya, and in the inner ether He is the wonderful Light which is the

1. Tat is apparently here treated as in the objective case agreeing, with vareṇyaṁ, etc., but others holding that the vyāhṛti (Bhūr-bhuvah-svah) form part of and should be linked with, the rest of the Gāyatrī treat tat as part of a genitive compound connected with the previous vyahṛti, in which case it is teshām.

2. It may, however, be said that yat is there in Yo nah.

Smokeless Fire. In short, that Being whom the sādhaka realizes in the region of his heart is the Āditya in the heavenly firmament. The two are one. The word is derived in two ways: (1) from the root bhrij, "ripen, mature, destroy, reveal, shine." In this derivation Sūrya is He who matures and transforms all things. He Himself shines and reveals all things by His light. And it is He who at the final Dissolution (pralaya) will in His image of destructive Fire (kālāgnī), destroy all things. (2) From bha = dividing all things into different classes; ra = colour; for He produces the colour of all created objects; ga, constantly going and returning. The sun divides all things, produces the different colours of all things, and is constantly going and returning. As the Brāhmaṇa-sarvasva says: "The Bhargah is the Ātmā of all that exists, whether moving or motionless, in the three lokas (Bhūr-bhuvah-svah). There is nothing which exists apart from it."

Devasya is the genitive of Deva, agreeing with Savituh. Deva is the radiant and playful (līlāmaya) one, Sūrya, is in constant play with creation (sṛṣṭi), existence (sthiti), and destruction (pralaya), and by His radiance pleases all. (Līlā, as applied to the Brahman, is the equivalent of māyā.) Vareṇyam = varaṇīya, or adorable. He should be meditated upon and adored that we may be relieved of the misery of birth and death. Those who fear rebirth, who desire freedom from death and liberation and who strive to escape the three kinds of pain (tāpa-traya), which are ādhyātmika, ādhidaivika, and ādhibhautika, meditate upon and adore the Bharga, who, dwelling in the region of the Sun, is Himself the three regions called Bhūr-loka, Bhuvar-loka, and Svar-loka. Dhīmahi=dhyāyema, from the root dhyai. We meditate upon, or let us meditate upon.

Pracodayāt = may He direct. The Gāyatrī does not so expressly state, but it is understood that such direction is along the catur-varga, or four-fold path, which is dharma, artha, kāma, and mokṣa (piety, wealth, desire and its fulfilment, and liberation, *vide post*). The Bhargah is ever directing our inner faculties (buddhi-vṛtti) along these paths.

The above is the Vaidik Gāyatrī, which, according to the Vaidik system, none but the twice-born may utter. To the Śūdra whether man or woman, and to women of all other castes it is forbidden. The Tantra, which has Gāyatrī-Mantra of its own, shows no such exclusiveness; Mahānirvāṇa-Tantra, Chapter III, verses 109-111, gives the Brahma-gāyatrī for worshippers of the Brahman: "Parameśvarāya vidmahe; para-tattvāya dhīmahi; tan no Brahma pracodayāt" (May we know the supreme Lord, Let us contemplate the Supreme essence. And may that Brahmah direct us).[1]

## YANTRA

This word in its most general sense means an instrument, or that by which anything is accomplished. In worship it is that by which the mind is fixed on its object. The Yoginī-Tantra says that the Devī should be worshipped either in pratimā (image), maṇḍala,[2] or yantra.[3] At a certain stage of spiritual progress the sādhaka is qualified to worship yantra. The siddha-yogi in inward worship (antar-pūjā) commences with the worship of yantra which is the sign (saṁketa) of brahma-vijñāna as the mantra is the

1. "The Great Liberation".

2. A figure frequently drawn or made with various colours. The difference between a mandala and a yantra is that the former is used in the case of any Devata, whereas, a yantra is appropriate to a specific Devata only.

3. Or where these are not available then in other substances, such as water, the flowers aparājitā, jabā, karavīra, droṇa, etc. (Kaulāvaliya-Tantra).

saṁketa of the Devatā. It is also said that yantra is so called because it subdues (niyantrana) lust, anger, and the other sins of jīva and the sufferings caused thereby.[1]

The yantra is a diagram engraved or drawn on metal, paper, or other substances,[2] which is worshipped in the same manner as an image (pratimā). As different mantras are prescribed for different worships, so are different yantras. The yantras are therefore of various designs, according to the object of worship.[3] The cover of this work shows a Gāyatrī yantra belonging to the author. In the centre triangle are engraved in the middle the words, Śrī Śrī Gāyatrī sva-prasāda siddhiṁ kuru ("Śrī Śrī Gāyatrī Devī: grant me success"), and at each inner corner there are the bījas, Hrīṁ and Hrah. In the spaces formed by the intersections of the outer ovoid circles is the bīja "Hrīṁ". The outside circular band contains the bīja "Tha" which indicates "Svāhā", commonly employed to terminate the feminine mantra or vidyā. The eight lotus petals which spring from the band are inscribed with the bīja, "Hrīṁ, Iṁ, Hraḥ". The outermost band contains all the mātṛkas, or letters of the alphabet, from akāra to kṣa.[4] The whole is enclosed in the way common to all yantras by a bhūpura, by which, as it were, the yantra is enclosed from the outer world.[5] The yantra when inscribed with mantra, serves (so far as these are concerned) the purpose of a mnemonic

1. "Principles of Tantra", (Sādhāraṇa-upāsanā-tattva).

2. Thus the magical treatises speak of yantra designed on leopards' and donkeys' skin, human bones, etc.

3. A considerable number are figured in the Tantrasāra.

4. In this and other metal yantras no figures of Devatā are shown. These not uncommonly appear in yantras drawn or printed on paper, such as the eight Bhairava Śakti, etc.

5. In painted yantra serpents are commonly shown crawling outside the bhū-pura.

chart of the mantra appropriate to the particular Devatā whose presence is to be invoked into the yantra. Certain preliminaries precede, as in the case of a pratimā, the worship of a yantra. The worshipper first meditates upon the Devatā, and then arouses Him or Her in himself. He then communicates the divine presence thus aroused to the yantra. When the Devatā has by the appropriate mantra been invoked into the yantra, the vital airs (prāṇa) of the Devatā are infused therein by the prāṇa-pratiṣṭhā ceremony, mantra, and mudrā. The Devatā is thereby installed in the yantra,[1] which is no longer mere gross matter veiling the spirit which has been always there, but instinct with its aroused presence, which the sādhaka first welcomes and then worships. Mantra in itself is Devatā, and yantra is mantra in that it is the body of the Devatā who is mantra.[2]

## MUDRĀ

The term mudrā is derived from the root mud, "to please," and in its upāsana form is so called because it gives pleasure to the Devas. Devānāṁ moda-dā mudrā tasmāt taṁ yatnataścaret. It is said that there are 108, of which 55 are commonly used.[3] The term means ritual gestures made with the hands in worship or positions of the body in yoga practice. Thus of the first class the matsya-(fish) mudrā is formed in offering arghya by placing the right hand on the back of the left and extending, fish-like, on each side the two thumbs, with the object that the conch which

---

1. See, e.g., Mahā-nirvāṇā-Tantra, chap. vi, verses 63 *et seq.* The process is the same as that employed in the case of images (pratimā).

2. Yantram mantram-mayaṁ proktaṁ mantrātmā devataiva hi.
Dehātmanor-yathi bhedo, yantra-devatayostathā (Kaulāvaliya Tantra).

3. Śabda-kalpa-druma—*sub voc* mudrā, and see chap. xi Nirvāṇa Tantra. As to the special sense of mudrā in pāncatattva, *vide post sub voc.*

contains water may be regarded as an ocean with aquatic animals; and the yoni-mudrā which presents that organ as a triangle formed by the thumbs, the two first fingers, and the two little fingers is shown with the object of invoking the Devī to come and take Her place before the worshipper, the yoni being considered to be Her pīṭhā or yantra. The upāsana mudrā is thus nothing but the outward expression of inner resolve which it at the same time intensifies. Mudrās are employed in worship (arcana), japa, dhyānā (*q.v.*), kāmya-karma (rites done to effect particular objects), pratiṣṭhā (*q.v.*), snāna (bathing), āvāhana (welcoming), naivedya (offering of food), and visarjana, or dismissal of the Devatā. Some mudrās of hatha yoga are described *sub voc,* "Yoga". The Gheraṇḍa-saṁhitā[1] says that knowledge of the yoga mudrās grants all siddhis, and that their performance produces physical benefits such as stability, firmness, and cure of disease.

## SAMDHYĀ

The Vaidiki saṁdhyā is the rite performed by the twice-born castes thrice a day, at morning, midday, and evening. The morning saṁdhyā is preceded by the following acts. On awakening, a mantra is said in invocation of the Tri-mūrti and the sun, moon, and planets, and salutation is made to the Guru. The Hindu dvi-ja then recites the mantra: "I am a Deva. I am indeed the sorrowless Brahman. By nature I am eternally free, and in the form of existence, intelligence, and bliss." He then offers the actions of the day to the Deity, confesses his inherent frailty,[2] and prays that he may do right. Then, leaving his

---

1. Chapter III, verses 4, 8, 10.

2. "I know dharma and yet would not do it. I know adharma, and yet would not renounce it." The Hindu form of the common experience—*Video meliora proboque; deteriora sequor.*

bed and touching the earth with his right foot, the dvi-ja says, "Oṁ, O Earth! salutation to Thee, the Guru of all that is good." After attending to natural calls, the twice-born does ācamana (sipping of water) with mantra, cleanses his teeth, and takes his early morning[1] bath to the accompaniment of mantra. He then puts on his caste-mark (tilaka) and makes tarpaṇam, or oblation of water, to the Deva, Ṛṣi and Pitṛ. The saṁdhyā follows, which consists of ācamana (sipping of water), mārjana-snānam (sprinkling of the whole body with water taken with the hand or kuśa-grass), prāṇāyāma (regulation of prāṇa through its manifestation in breath), agha-marṣaṇa (expulsion of the person of sin from the body; the prayer to the sun, and then (the canon of the saṁdhyā) the silent recitation (japa) of the Gāyatrī-mantra, which consists of invocation (āvāhana) of the Gāyatrī-Devī; ṛṣi-nyāsa and ṣadāṅganyāsā (*vide post*), meditation on the Devī-Gāyatrī in the morning as Brahmanī; at midday as Vaiṣṇavī; and in the evening as Rudrāṇī; japa of the Gāyatrī a specified number of times; dismissal (visarjana) of the Devī, followed by other mantras.[2]

Besides the Brahmanical Vaidikī-saṁdhyā from which the Śūdras are debarred, there is the Tāntriki-saṁdhyā, which may be performed by all. The general outline is similar; the rite is simpler; the mantras vary; and the Tāntrika-bījas or "seed" mantras are employed.

---

1. The householder is required to bathe twice, the ascetic at each of the three saṁdhyas.

2. The above is a general outline of the Sāma Veda saṁdhyā, though as each Hindu is of a particular sect and Veda, the saṁdhyā differs in detail. See Kriyākāṇḍavāridhi and the Purohita-darpaṇa, and Śrīśa Chandra-Vasu, "Daily Practice of the Hindus." The positions and mudrā are illustrated in Mrs. S. C. Belnos' "Saṁdhyā or Daily Prayer of the Brahmin" (1831).

## PŪJĀ

This word is the common term for worship of which there are numerous synonyms in the Sanskrit language.[1] Pūjā is done daily of the Iṣṭa-devatā or the particular Deity worshipped by the sādhaka—the Devī in the case of a Śākta, Viṣṇu in the case of a Vaiṣṇava, and so forth. But though the Iṣṭa-devatā is the principal object of worship, yet in pūjā all worship the Panca-devatā, or the Five Devās—Āditya (the Sun), Gaṇeśa, the Devī, Śiva, and Viṣṇu or Nārāyaṇa. After worship of the Pancadevatā the family Deity (Kula-devatā), who is generally the same as the Iṣṭa-devatā, is worshipped. Pūjā, which is kāmya, or done to gain a particular end as also vrata, are preceded by the saṁkalpa; that is, a statement of the resolution to do the worship; as also of the particular object, if any, with which it is done.[2]

There are sixteen upacāras, or things done or used in pūjā: (1) āsana (seat of the image); (2) svāgata (welcome); (3) pādya (water for washing the feet); (4) arghya (offering of unboiled rice, flowers, sandal paste, durva grass,[3] etc., to the Devatā in the kushī) (vessel); (5 and 6) ācamana (water for sipping, which is offered twice); (7) madhuparka (honey, ghee, milk, and curd offered in a silver or brass vessel); (8) snāna (water for bathing); (9) vasana (cloth); (10) ābharana (jewels); (11) gandha (scent and sandal paste is given); (12) puṣpa (flowers); (13) dhūpa (incense stick); (14) dīpa (light); (15) naivedya (food); (16) van-

---

1. Such as arcanā, vandanā, saparyyā, arhanā, namasyā, arcā, bhajanā, etc.

2. It runs in the form: "I—of gotra—etc., am about to perform this pūjā (or vrata) with the object," etc.

3. Kuśa grass is used only in pitṛ-kriyā or śrāddha, and in homa. Arghya is of two kinds—sāmanya (general), and viśeṣa (special).

dana or namas-kāra (prayer). Other articles are used which vary with the pūjā, such as Tulasī leaf in the Viṣṇu-pūja and bæl-(bilva) leaf in the Śiva-pūja. The mantras said also vary according to the worship. The seat (āsana) of the worshipper is purified. Salutation being made to the Śakti of support or the sustaining force (ādhāra-śakti), the water, flowers, etc., are purified. All obstructive spirits are driven away (Bhūtāpasarpaṇa), and the ten quarters are fenced from their attack by striking the earth three times with the left foot, uttering the Astra-bīja "phat", and by snapping the fingers (twice) round the head. Prāṇāyāma (regulation of breath) is performed and (*vide post*) the elements of the body are purified (bhūta-suddhi). There is nyāsa (*vide post*); dhyāna (meditation); offering of the upacāra; japa (*vide post*), prayer and obeisance (praṇāma). In the aṣṭa-mūrtī-pūjā of Śiva, the Deva is worshipped under the eight forms: Śarva (Earth), Bhava (Water), Rudra (Fire), Ugra (Air), Bhīma (Ether), Paśupati (yajamāna—the Sacrificer man), Iśana (Sun), Mahādeva (Moon).[1]

## YAJÑA

This word, which comes from the root yaj (to worship), is commonly translated "sacrifice". The Sanskrit word is, however, retained in the translation, since Yajña means other things also than those which come within the meaning of the word "sacrifice", as understood by an English reader. Thus the "five great sacrifices" (panca-mahā-yajña) which should be performed daily by the Brāhmaṇa are: The homa[2] sacrifice, including Vaiśva-deva offering;[3] bhūta-

1. See Chapter V of Toḍala-Tantra.

2. *Vide post.*

3. Offerings of food and other things are made in the domestic fire. (See Krīya-kāṇḍa-vāridhi, p. 917).

yajña or bali, in which offerings are made to Devā, Bhūta, and other Spirits and to animals; pitṛ-yajña or tarpaṇa, oblations to the pitṛ; Brahma-yajña, or study of the Vedas and Manuṣyayajñā,[1] or entertainment of guests (atithisaparyā). By these five yajñas the worshipper places himself in right relations with all beings, affirming such relation between Deva, Pitṛ, Spirits, men, the organic creation, and himself.

Homa, or Deva-yajña, is the making of offerings to Fire, which is the carrier thereof to the Deva. A firepit (kuṇḍa) is prepared and fire when brought from the house of a Brāhmaṇa is consecrated with mantra. The fire is made conscious with the mantra—Vaṁ vahni-caitanyāya namah, and then saluted and named. Meditation is then made on the three nādīs (*vide ante*)—Idā, Piṅgalā, and Suṣumnā—and on Agni, the Lord of Fire. Offerings are made to the Iṣṭa-devatā in the fire. After the pūjā of fire, salutation is given as in Ṣaḍaṅga-nyāsa, and then clarified butter (ghee) is poured with a wooden spoon into the fire with mantra, commencing with Oṁ and ending with Svāhā. Homa is of various kinds,[2] several of which are referred to in the text, and is performed either daily, as in the case of the ordinary nitya-vaiśva-deva-homa, or on special occasions, such as the upanayana or sacred thread ceremony, marriage, vrata, and the like. It is of various kinds, such as prāyaścitta-homa, sṛṣtikṛt-homā, janu-homa, dhārā homa, and others, some of which will be found in the text.

Besides the yajña mentioned there are others. Manu speaks of four kinds: deva, bhauta (where articles and ingredients are employed, as in the case of homa, daiva,

---

1. Also called Nṛi-yajña (man sacrifice).

2. See Kriyā-kāṇḍa-vāridhi, p. 133. Homa may be either Vaidīk, Paurānik, or Tāntrik.

bali), nṛyajña, and pitṛ-yajña. Others are spoken of, such as japa-yajña, dhyāna-yajña, etc. Yajñas are also classified according to the dispositions and intentions of the worshipper into sātvika, rājasika, and tāmasika yajña.

## VRATA

Vrata is a part of Naimittika, or voluntary karma.[1] It is that which is the cause of virtue (puṇya), and is done to achieve its fruit. Vratas are of various kinds. Some of the chief are Janmāṣṭamī on Kṛṣṇa's birthday; Śivarātri in honour of śiva; and the ṣatpañcamī, Durvāṣtami, Tālanavamī; Anantacaturdaśī performed at specified times in honour of Lakshmi Nārāyaṇa, and Ananta. Others may be performed at any time, such as the Sāvitrī-vrata by women only,[2] and the Kārtikeya-pūjā by men only.[3] The great vrata is the celebrated Durgā-pūjā, mahā-vrata in honour of the Devī as Durgā, which will continue as long as the sun and moon endure, and which, if once commenced, must always be continued. There are numerous other vratas which have developed to a great extent in Bengal, and for which there is no Śāstric authority such as Madhu-saṁkrānti-vrata, Jalasaṁkrāntivrata, and others. While each vrata has its peculiarities, certain features are common to vratas of differing kinds. There is both in preparation and performance saṁyama, such as sexual continence, eating of particular food such as haviṣyānnā,[4] fasting, bathing. No flesh or fish taken. The mind is concentrated to its pur-

1. *Vide ante.*

2. To attain good wifehood, long life for the husband in this world, and life with him in the next.

3. To secure children.

4. To prepare haviṣyānnā, particular kinds of fruit and vegetable such as green bananas, dāl, sweet potatoes (lāl ālu, in the vernacular), together with the unboiled rice are placed in one pot. Only so much water is poured

poses, and the vow or resolution (niyama) is taken. Before the vrata the Sun, Planets, and Kula-devatā are worshipped, and by the "sūryah-somoyamah-kāla" mantra all Devas and Beings are invoked to the side of the worshipper. In the vaidika vrata the saṁkalpa[1] is made in the morning, and the vrata is done before midday.

## TAPAS

This term is generally translated as meaning penance or austerities. It includes these, such as the four monthly fasts (cātur-māsya), the sitting between five fires (pancāgnitapah), and the like. It has, however, also a wider meaning, and in this wider sense is of three kinds, namely, śarīra, or bodily; vācika, by speech; mānasa, in mind. The first includes external worship, reverence, and support given to the Guru, Brāhmaṇas, and the wise (prājña), bodily cleanliness, continence, simplicity of life and avoidance of hurt to any being (ahiṁsā). The second form includes truth, good, gentle, and affectionate speech, and the study of the Vedas. The third or mental tapas includes self-restraint, purity of disposition, silence, tranquillity, and silence. Each of these classes has three subdivisions, for tapas may be sātvika, rājasika, or tāmasika, according as it is done with faith, and without regard to its fruit; or for its fruit; or is done through pride and to gain honour and respect; or, lastly, which is done ignorantly or with a view to injure and destroy others, such as the sādhana of the Tān-

---

in as is necessary to make the whole boil. It should be boiled until no water is left. After the pot is taken off the fire, ghee and salt are added.

1. *Vide ante*, p. 96.

trika-ṣat-karma,[1] when performed for a malevolent purpose (abhicāra).

## JAPA

Japa is defined as "vidhānena mantroccāraṇam", or the repeated utterance or recitation of mantra according to certain rules.[2] It is according to the Tantrasāra of three kinds: Vācika or verbal japa, in which the mantra is audibly recited, the fifty mātṛkās being sounded nasally with bindu; Upāṁśu-japa, which is superior to the last kind, and in which the tongue and lips are moved, but no sound, or only a slight whisper, is heard; and, lastly, the highest form which is called mānasa-japa, or mental utterance. In this there is neither sound nor movement of the external organs, but a repetition in the mind which is fixed on the meaning of the mantra. One reason given for the differing values attributed to the several forms is that where there is audible utterance the mind thinks of the words and the process of correct utterance, and is therefore to a greater (as in the case of vācika-japa), or to a less degree (as in the case of upāṁśujapa), distracted from a fixed attention to the meaning of the mantra. The Japas of different kinds have also the relative values attachable to thought and its materialization in sound and word. Certain conditions are prescribed as

---

1. Śānti, Vaśīkarana, Stambhana, Vidveṣaṇa, Uccātana and Māraṇa.

See Indra-jāla-vidyā; the Kāmaratna of Nāga-bhaṭṭa; Ṣat-karmadīpikā of Śrī-Kṛṣṇa Vidyā-vāgīśa Bhattācārya, Siddha-yogesvari-Tantra, Siddha-Nāgārjuna, Kakṣa-puta, Phet-kāriṇī, and other Tantras (*passim*).

2. Though mere book knowledge is, according to the Ṣat-karmadīpikā, useless.

> Pustake likitā vidyâ yena sundari japyate,
> Siddhir na jāyate devi kalpa-koti-śatair api.

those under which japa should be done, relating to physical cleanliness, the dressing of the hair, and wearing of silk garments, the seat (āsana), the avoidance of certain conditions of mind and actions, and the nature of the recitation. The japa is useless unless done a specified number of times of which 108 is esteemed to be excellent. The counting is done either with a mālā or rosary (mālā-japa), or with the thumb of the right hand upon the joints of the fingers of that hand (kara-japa). The method of the counting in the latter case may differ according to the mantra.[1]

## SAMSKĀRA

There are ten (or, in the case of Śūdras, nine) purificatory ceremonies, or "sacraments," called saṁskāras, which are done to aid and purify the jīva in the important events of his life. These are jīva-sheka, also called garbhādhāna-ṛtu-saṁskāra, performed after menstruation, with the object of insuring and sanctifying conception. The garbhādhāna ceremony takes place in the daytime on the fifth day and qualifies for the real garbhādhāna at night—that is, the placing of the seed in the womb. It is preceded on the first day by the ṛtu-saṁskāra, which is mentioned in Chapter IX of Mahānirvāṇa-Tantra. After conception and during pregnancy, the puṁ-savana and sīmantonnayana rites are performed; the first upon the wife perceiving the signs of conception, and the second during the fourth, sixth, or eighth month of pregnancy.

In the ante-natal life there are three main stages, whether viewed from the objective (physical) standpoint, or from the subjective (super-physical) standpoint.[2] The

1. See as to Japa, Tantrasāra, 75, *et seq.*

2. For what follows on the medical side, see the Appendix, vol. i, p. 194, on the Saṁskāras, by Dr. Louise Appel, in the "Praṇava-vāda" of Bhagavān Dās.

first period includes on the physical side all the structural and physiological changes which occur in the fertilized ovum from the moment of fertilization until the period when the embryonic body, by the formation of trunk, limbs, and organs, is fit for the entrance of the individualized life, or jīvātmā. When the pronuclear activity and differentiation are completed, the jīvātmā, whose connection with the pronuclei initiated the pronuclear or formative activity, enters the miniature human form, and the second stage of growth and development begins. The second stage is the fixing of the connection between the jīva and the body, or the rendering of the latter viable. This period includes all the anatomical and physiological modifications by which the embryonic body becomes a viable fœtus. With the attainment of viability, the stay of the jīva has been assured; physical life is possible for the child, and the third stage in ante-natal life is entered. Thus, on the form side, if the language of comparative embryology is used, the first saṁskāra denotes the impulse to development, from the "fertilization of the ovum" to the "critical period". The second saṁskāra denotes the impulse to development from the "critical period" to that of the "viability stage of the fœtus"; and the third saṁskāra denotes the development from "viability" to "full term".

On the birth of the child there is the jāta-karma, performed for the continued life of the new-born child. Then follows the nāma-karaṇa, or naming ceremony, and niṣkrāmaṇa in the fourth month after delivery, when the child is taken out of doors for the first time and shown the sun, the vivifying source of life, the material embodiment of the Divine Savitā. Between the fifth and eighth month after birth the annaprāśana ceremony is observed, when rice is put in the child's mouth for the first time. Then follows the cūda-karaṇa, or tonsure ceremony;[1] and in the case of the first three or "twice-born" classes, upanayana, or investiture with the sacred thread. Herein the jīva is reborn into spiritual life. There is, lastly, udvāha, or marriage, whereby the unperfected jīva insures through offspring that continued human life which is the condition of its progress and ultimate return to its Divine Source. These are all described in the Ninth Chapter of this Tantra. There are also ten saṁskāras of the mantra (*q.v.*). The saṁskāras are intended to be performed at certain stages in the development of the human body, with the view to effect results beneficial to the human organism. Medical science of to-day seeks to reach the same results, but uses for this purpose the physical methods of modern Western science, suited to an age of materiality; whereas in the saṁskāras the superphysical (psychic, or occult, or metaphysical and subjective) methods of ancient Eastern science are employed. The sacraments of the Catholic Church and others of its ceremonies, some of which have now fallen into disuse,[2] are Western examples of the same psychic method.

## PURAŚCARANA

This form of sādhana consists in the repetition (after certain preparations and under certain conditions) of a mantra a large number of times. The ritual[3] deals with the time and place of performance, the measurements and decorations of the maṇḍapa, or pandal, and of the altar and

1. A lock of hair is left at the top of the head, called śikhā. As when a king visits a place, the royal banner is set up, so on the head in whose thousand-petalled lotus the Brahman resides, the śikhā is left.

2. E.g., the blessing of the marital bed, which bears analogy to the Hindu garbhādhāna rite.

3. For a short account, see Puraścaraṇa-bodhinī, by Hara-kumāra-Tagore (1895), and see Tantrasāra, p. 71.

similar matters. There are certain rules as to food both prior to, and during, its performance. The sādhaka should eat haviṣyānna,[1] or alternately boiled milk (kṣīra), fruits, or Indian vegetables, or anything obtained by begging, and avoid all food calculated to influence the passions. Certain conditions and practices are enjoined for the destruction of sin, such as continence, bathing, japa (*q.v.*) of the Sāvitrī-mantra 5008, 3008, or 1008 times, the entertainment of Brāhmaṇas, and so forth. Three days before pūjā there is worship of Gaṇeśa and Kṣetra-pāla, Lord of the Place. Pañca-gavya,[2] or the five products of the cow, are eaten. The Sun, Moon, and Devas, are invoked. Then follows the saṁkalpa.[3] The ghata, or kalaśa (jar), is then placed into which the Devī is to be invoked. A maṇḍala or figure of a particular design is marked on the ground, and on it the ghata is placed. Then the five or nine gems are placed on the kalaśa, which is painted with red and covered with leaves. The ritual then prescribes for the tying of the crown lock (śikhā), the posture (āsana) of the sādhaka, japa (*q.v.*), nyāsa (*q.v.*), and the mantra ritual or process. There is meditation, as directed. Kulluka[4] is said and the mantra "awakened" (mantra-caitanya), and recited the number of times for which the vow has been taken.

## BHUTA-ŚUDDHI

The object of this ritual, which is described in Mahānirvāṇa-Tantra, Chapter V, verses 93 *et seq,* is the purification of the elements of which the body is composed.[5]

---

1. See p. 99. note 4.

2. Milk, curd, ghee, urine, and dung the two last (except in the case of the pious) in smaller quantity.

3. See p. 96. *ante.*

4. See p. 87, *ante.*

5. And not "removal of evil demons" as Professor Monier Williams's Dictionary has it.

The Mantra-mahodadhi speaks of it as a rite which is preliminary to the worship of a Deva.[1] The process of evolution from the Para-brahman has been described. By this ritual a mental process of involution takes place whereby the body is in thought resolved into the source from whence it has come. Earth is associated with the sense of smell, water with taste, fire with sight, air with touch, and ether with sound. Kuṇḍalinī is roused and led to the svādhiṣṭhāna Cakra. The "earth" element is dissolved by that of "water," as "water" is by "fire," "fire" by "air," and "air" by "ether." This is absorbed by a higher emanation, and that by a higher, and so on, until the Source of all is reached. Having dissolved each gross element (mahā-bhūta), together with the subtle element (tanmātra) from which it proceeds, and the connected organ of sense (indriya) by another, the worshipper absorbs the last element, "ether," with the tanmātra sound into self-hood (ahaṁkāra), the latter into Mahat, and that, again, into Prakṛti, thus retracing the steps of evolution. Then, in accordance with the monistic teaching of the Vedānta, Prakṛti is Herself thought of as the Brahman, of which She is the energy, and with which, therefore, She is already one. Thinking then of the black Puruṣa, which is the image of all sin, the body is purified by mantra,. accompanied by kumbhaka and recaka,[2] and the sādhaka meditates upon the new celestial (devā) body, which has thus been made and which is then strengthened by a "celestial gaze."[3]

## NYĀSA

This word, which comes from the root "to place," means placing the tips of the fingers and palm of the right

---

1. Taraṅga i.:

   Devārcā-yogyatā-prāptyai bhūta-suddhiṁ samācaret.

2. See Prāṇāyāma, *sub. voc.* Yoga post.

3. *Vide post.*

hand on various parts of the body, accompanied by particular mantra; The nyāsas are of various kinds.[1] Jīva-nyāsa[2] follows upon bhūta-śuddhi. After the purification of the old, and the formation of the celestial body, the sādhaka proceeds by jīva-nyāsa to infuse the body with the life of the Devī. Placing his hand on his heart, he says the "soham̐" mantra ("I am He"), thereby identifying himself with the Devī. Then, placing the eight Kula-kuṇḍalinīs in their several places, he says the following mantra: Ām̐, Krīm̐, Klīm̐, Yam̐, Ram̐, Lam̐, Vam̐, Sam̐, Hom̐, Śam̐, Ṣam̐, Haum̐, Ham̐sah: the vital airs of the highly blessed and auspicious Primordial Kālikā are here.[3] "Ām̐, etc., the embodied spirit of the highly blessed and auspicious Kālikā is placed here."[4] "Ām̐, etc., here are all the senses of the highly auspicious and blessed Kālikā;"[5] and, lastly, "Ām̐, etc., may the speech, mind, sight, hearing, smell, and vital airs of the highly blessed and auspicious Kālikā coming here always abide here in peace and happiness Svāhā."[6] The sādhaka then becomes devatā-maya. After having thus dissolved the sinful body, made a new Deva body, and infused it with the life of the Devī, he proceeds to mātṛkānyāsa. Mātṛkā are the fifty letters of the Sanskrit alphabet; for as from a mother comes birth, so from mātṛkā, or sound, the world proceeds. Śabdabrahman, the "Sound," "Logos," or "Word," is the Creator of the worlds of name and of form.

---

1. See Kriya-kānda-vāridhi (p. 120, chap. ii et seq.).

2. See Mahānirvāṇa-Tantra, Chapter V, verse 105, where a fuller account is given of the above.

3. Śrimad-ādyākalikāyāh prānā iha prānāh.

4. Śrimad-ādya-Kālikāyāh jīva iha sthitah.

5. Śrimad-ādyā-kālikāyāh sarvendrīyāni sthitāni.

6. Śrimad - ādyā - kālikāyāh vāṅg - manaś - cakṣuh - śrotrajihvāghrāṇa - prānāh iha - gatya sukham̐ ciram̐ tiṣṭhantu svāhā.

The bodies of the Devatā are composed of the fifty mātṛkas. The sādhaka, therefore, first sets mentally (antar-mātṛkā-nyāsa) in their several places in the six cakras, and then externally by physical action (Bāhyamātṛkānyāsa) the letters of the alphabet which form the different parts of the body of the Devatā, which is thus built up in the sādhaka himself. He places his hand on different parts of his body, uttering distinctly at the same time the appropriate mātṛkā for that part.

The mental disposition in the cakras is as follows: In the Ajña Lotus, Haṁ, Kṣaṁ, (each letter in this and the succeeding cases is said, followed by the mantra namah);[1] in the Viśuddha Lotus Aṁ, Āṁ, and the rest of the vowels; in the Anāhata Lotus kaṁ, khaṁ to thaṁ; in the maṇi-pūra Lotus, daṁ, dham, etc., to pham; in the Svādhiṣṭhāna Lotus bam, bham to laṁ; and, lastly, in the Mūlādhāra Lotus, vaṁ, śaṁ,[2] ṣaṁ,[3] saṁ. The external disposition then follows. The vowels in their order with anusvāra and visarga are placed on the forehead, face, right and left eye, right and left ear, right and left nostril, right and left cheek, upper and lower lip, upper and lower teeth, head, and hollow of the mouth. The consonants kaṁ to vaṁ are placed on base of right arm and the elbow, wrist, base and tips of fingers, left arm, right and left leg, right and left side, back, navel, belly, heart, right and left shoulder, space between the shoulders (kakuda), and then from the heart to the right palm Śaṁ is placed; and from the heart to the left palm the (second) ṣaṁ; from the heart to the right foot, saṁ; from the heart to the left foot, haṁ; and, lastly, from the heart to the belly, and from the heart to

1. Thus, Haṁ namah, Kṣaṁ namah etc.

2. Tālavya śa—soft, palatal, sh.

3. Mūrdhanya ṣa—hard cerebral sh.

the mouth, kṣaṁ. In each case oṁ is said at the beginning and namah at the end. According to the Tantrasāra, mātṛkā-nyāsa is also classified into four kinds, performed with different aims—viz: kevala where the mātṛka is pronounced without bindu; bindu-saṁyuta with bindu; saṁsarga with visarga; and sobhya with visarga and bindu.

Ṛṣi-nyāsa then follows for the attainment of the caturvarga.[1] The assignment of the mantra is to the head, mouth, heart, anus, the two feet, and all the body generally. The mantras commonly employed are: "In the head, salutation to the Ṛṣī (Revealer) Brahmā;[2] in the mouth, salutation to the mantra Gāyatrī;[3] in the heart, salutation to the Devī Mother Sarasvatī;[4] in the hidden part, salutation to the bīja, the consonants;[5] salutation to the śakti, the vowels in the feet;[6] salutation to visargah, the kīlaka in the whole body."[7] Another form in which the bīja is employed is that of the Ādyā: it is referred to but not given in Chap. V, verse 123, and is: "In the head, salutation to Brahmā and the Brahmarṣis;[8] in the mouth, salutation to Gāyatrī and the other forms of verse;[9] in the heart salutation to the primordial Devatā Kālī;[10] in the hidden part, salutation to the bīja, krīṁ;"[11] in the two feet, salutation to

---

1. Dharmārtha-kāma-mokṣaye ṛṣi-nyāse viniyogah.
2. Śirasi Brahmarṣaye namah.
3. Mukhe Gāyatryai-cchandase namah.
4. Hṛdaye mātṛkāyai sarasvatyai devatāyai namah.
5. Guhye (that is, the anus) vyañjanāya bījāya namah.
6. pādayoh svarebhyah śaktibhyo namah.
7. Sarvāṅgeṣu visargāya kīlakāya (that is, that which comes at the end or closes; the hard breathing) namah.
8. Śirasi brahmaṇe brahmarṣibhyo namah.
9. Muke gāyatryādibhyaścandobhyo namah.
10. Hṛdaye ādyāyai kālikāyai devatāyai namah.
11. Guhye krīṁ-bijāya namah.

the śakti, Hrīm;[1] in all the body, salutation to the Kālikā Śrīm."[2]

Then follows aṅga-nyāsa and kara-nyāsa. These are both forms of ṣadanga-nyāsa.[3] When ṣadaṅga-nyāsa is performed on the body, it is called hṛdayādi-ṣadanga nyāsa; and when done with the five fingers and palms of the hands only, aṅguṣṭhādi ṣadanga-nyāsa. The consonants of the ka-varga group, and the long vowel ā are reçited with "hṛdayāya namāh" (salutation to the heart). The short vowel i, the consonants of the ca-varga group, and the long vowel ī, are said with "śirasī svāhā" (svāhā to the head). The hard ta-varga consonants set between the two vowels u and ū are recited with "śikhāyai vaṣat" (vaṣat to the crown lock); similarly the soft ta-varga between the vowels e and ai are said with "kavacāya[4] hum." The short vowel o, the pavarga, and the long vowel o are recited with netra-trayāya vauṣat (vauṣat to the three eyes).[5] Lastly, between bindu and visarga[6] the consonants ya to kṣa with "karatala-kara pṛṣṭhābhyāṁ astrāya phat" (phat to the front and back of the palm).[7]

The mantras of ṣadanga-nyāsa on the body are used for kara-nyāsa, in which they are assigned to the thumbs,

---

1. Pādayoh krīm-śaktaye namah.

2. Sarvāngeṣu śrīṁ-kālikāyai namah.

3. Ṣat (six), aṅga (limb), nyāsa (placing).

4. The kavaca is the arms crossed on the chest, the hands clasping the upper part of the arms just beneath the shoulders.

5. Including the central eye of wisdom (jñana-cakṣu)

6. The nasal sound and hard breathing.

7. In all cases the letters are sounded with the nasal anusvâra, as (in the last) aṁ, yaṁ, raṁ, laṁ, vaṁ, aṁ, ṣaṁ, saṁ, haṁ, kshaṁ, ah, etc.

the "threatening" or index fingers, the middle fingers, the fourth, little fingers, and the front and back of the palm.

These actions on the body, fingers, and palms also stimulate the nerve centres and nerves therein.

In pītha-nyāsa, the pīthas are established in place of the mātṛka. The pīthas, in their ordinary sense, are Kāma-rūpa and the other places, a list of which is given in the Yoginī-hṛdaya.[1]

For the attainment of that state in which the sādhaka feels that the bhāva (nature, disposition) of the Devatā has come upon him, nyāsa is a great auxiliary. It is, as it were, the wearing of jewels on different parts of the body. The bīja of the Devatā are the jewels which the sādhaka places on the different parts of his body. By nyāsa he places his Abhīṣta-devatā in such parts, and by vyāpaka-nyāsa, he spreads its presence through himself. He becomes permeated by it losing himself in the divine Self.

Nyāsa is also of use in effecting the proper distribution of the śaktis of the human frame in their proper positions so as to avoid the production of discord and distraction in worship. Nyāsa as well as Āsana are necessary for the production of the desired state of mind and of cittaśuddhi (its purification). "Das denken ist der mass der Dinge."[2] Transformation of thought is Transformation of being. This is the essential principle and rational basis of all this and similar Tāntrik sādhanas.

---

1. See Bhāskara-rāya's Commentary on śloka 156 of the Lalitā-sahasra-nāma and *ante*. The number of Pithas is variously given as 50 or 51.

2. Prantl.

## PAÑCATATTVA

There are, as already stated, three classes of men—Paśu, Vīra, and Divya. The operation of the gunas which produce these types affect, on the gross material plane, the animal tendencies, manifesting in the three chief physical functions—eating and drinking, whereby the annamayakośa is maintained, and sexual intercourse, by which it is reproduced. These functions are the subject of the pañcatattva or pañcamakāra ("five m's"), as they are vulgarly called—viz.: madya (wine), māṁsa (meat), maṭsya (fish), mudrā (parched grain), and maithuna (coition). In ordinary parlance, mudrā means ritual gestures or positions of the body in worship and hathayoga, but as one of the five elements it is parched cereal, and is defined[1] as Bhriṣtadānyādikam: yadyad chavyanīyam prachakṣate; sā mudrā kathītā devi sarveshām naganandini. The Tantras speak of the five elements as pañcatattva, kuladravyā, kulatattva, and certain of the elements have esoteric names, such as kāraṇavāri or tirthavāri, for wine, the fifth element being usually called latāsadhana[2] (sādhana with woman, or śakti). The five elements, moreover have various meanings, according as they form part of the tāmasika (paśvācara), rājasika (vīrācāra), or divya or sāttvika sādhanas respectively.

All the elements or their substitutes are purified and consecrated, and then, with the appropriate ritual, the first four are consumed, such consumption being followed by latā-sādhana or its symbolic equivalent. The Tantra prohibits indiscriminate use of the elements, which may be consumed or employed only after purification (śodhana)

1. Yoginī-Tāntra (chap. vi).

2. "Creeper" to which woman, as clinging to the male tree, is likened.

and during worship[1] according to the Tāntric ritual. Then also, all excess is forbidden. The Śyāmā-rahasya says that intemperance leads to Hell, and this Tantra condemns it in Chapter V. A well-known saying in Tantra describes the true "hero" (vīra) to be, not he who is of great physical strength and prowess, the great eater and drinker, or man of powerful sexual energy, but he who has controlled his senses, is a truth-seeker, ever engaged in worship, and who has sacrificed lust and all other passions. (Jitendriyah, satyavādī, nityānuṣṭhānatatparāh, kāmādi-balidānaśca sa vīra iti gīyate)'.

The elements in their literal sense are not available in sādhana for all. The nature of the Paśu requires strict adherence to Vaidik rule in the matter of these physical functions even in worship. This rule prohibits the drinking of wine, a substance subject to the three curses of Brahma, Kaca, and Kṛṣṇa, in the following terms: Madyam apeyam adeyam agrāhyam ("Wine[2] must not be drunk, given, or taken"). The drinking of wine in ordinary life for satisfaction of the sensual appetite is, in fact, a sin, involving prāyascitta, and entailing, according to the Viṣṇu Purāṇa,[3] punishment in the same Hell as that to which a

---

1. See Tantrasāra, 698. citing Bhāva-cūdāmaṇī. As regards maithuna, the Bṛhānnila-Tantra (chap. iv) says: Paradārānna gaccheran gacchecca prajapedyadi (that is, for purpose of worship) and similarly the Uttara-Tantra:

Pūjākālaṁ vinā nānyaṁ puruṣāṁ manasā spṛset
Pujākāleca deveśī veśyeva paritoṣayet.

The same rule as regards both madya and maithuna is stated in the Kulāmṛta as elsewhere.

2. From the standpoint of Tāntrika-Virācāra, the drinking of wine here referred to is ordinary drinking, and not the ritual worship (of those qualified for it) with the purified substance which is Tārā (the Saviour) Herself in liquid form (dravamayī).

3. Viṣṇu-Purāṇa (Bk. II, chap. vi).

killer of a Brāhmaṇa goes. As regards flesh and fish, the higher castes (outside Bengal) who submit to the orthodox Smārtha discipline eat neither. Nor do high and strict Brāhmaṇas even in that Province. But the bulk of the people there, both men and women, eat fish, and men consume the flesh of male goats which have been previously offered to the Deity. The Vaidika dharma is equally strict upon the subject of sexual intercourse. Maithuna other than with the householder's own wife is condemned. And this is not only in its literal sense, but in that which is known as Aṣṭāṅga (eightfold) maithuna—viz., smaraṇam (thinking upon it), kīrttanam (talking of it), keli (play with women), prekṣaṇam (looking upon women), guhya-bhāṣaṇam (talk in private with women), saṁkalpa (wish or resolve for maithuna), adhyavasāya (determination towards it), kriyāniṣpati (actual accomplishment of the sexual act). In short, the paśu and except for ritual purposes those who are not paśus should, in the words of the Śāktakramīya, avoid maithuna, conversation on the subject, and assemblies of women (maithunam tatkathālāpaṁ tadgoṣṭhiṁ parivarjayet). Even in the case of the householder's own wife marital continency is enjoined. The divinity in woman, which the Tantra in particular proclaims, is also recognized in the ordinary Vaidik teaching, as must obviously be the case given the common foundation upon which all the Śāstras rest. Woman is not to be regarded merely as an object of enjoyment, but as a house-goddess (gṛhadevatā).[1] According to the sublime notions of Śruti, the union of man and wife is a veritable sacrificial rite—a sacrifice in fire (homa), wherein she is both hearth (kuṇḍa) and flame—and he who knows this as homa attains libera-

1. Cited in the Commentary on the Karpurādistotra (verse 15), by Mahāmahopādhyāya Kṛṣnanātha Nyāya-panchānana Bhatttāchāryya.

tion.[1] Similarly the Tāntrika-Mantra for the Śivaśakti Yoga runs: "This is the internal homa in which, by the path of suṣumnā, sacrifice is made of the functions of sense to the spirit as fire kindled with the ghee of merit and demerit taken from the mind as the ghee-pot Svāhā."[2] It is not only thus that wife and husband are associated, for the Vaidika-dharma (in this now neglected) prescribes that the householder should worship in company with his wife.[3] Brahmacarya, or continency, is not as is sometimes supposed, a requisite of the student āśrama only, but is a rule which governs the married householder (gṛhastha) also. According to Vaidika injunctions, union of man and wife must take place once a month on the fifth day after the cessation of the menses, and then only. Hence it is that the Nityā-Tantra when giving the characteristics of a paśu, says that he is one who avoids sexual union except on the fifth day (ṛtukālaṁvinā devī ramaṇaṁ parivrajayet). In other words, the paśu is he who in this case, as in other matters, follows for all purposes, ritual or otherwise, the Vaidik injunctions which govern the ordinary life of all.

The above-mentioned rules govern the life of all men. The only exception which the Tantra makes is for purpose of sādhana in the case of those who are competent (adhikāri) for vīrācāra. It is held, indeed, that the exception is not strictly an exception to Vaidik teaching at all and

---

1. See thirteenth mantra of the Homa-Prakaraṇa of the Bṛhadāraṇyaka-Upaniṣad. The Niruttara-Tantra (chap. i) says:

Yonirupā mahākāli śavah śayyā Prakīrtitā.
Smaśānam dvividhaṁ devi citā yonirmaheśvari.

2. Oṁ dharmādharma havirdīpte ātmāgnau manasā srucā. suṣumnā vartmanā nityam akṣavṛttirjuhomyahaṁ svāhā (Tantrasāra, 698, and see Prāṇatoṣinī).

3. Śastriko dharmamācaret (see also chap. xxxi of the Matsya-Śukta-Tantra).

that it is an error to suppose that the Tāntrika-rahasya-pūjā is opposed to the Vedas. Thus, whilst the Vaidik rule prohibits the use of wine in ordinary life and for purposes of mere sensual gratification it prescribes the religious yajña with wine. This ritual use the Tantra also allows, provided that the sādhaka is competent for the sādhana, in which its consumption is part of its ritual and method.

The Tantra enforces the Vaidik rule in all cases, ritual or otherwise, for those who are governed by the vaidikācāra. The Nityā-Tantra says: "They (paśu) should never worship the Devī during the latter part of the day, in the evening or at night" (rātrau naiva yajeddevīṁ saṁdhyāyāṁ vā parānhe); for all such worship connotes maithuna prohibited to the paśu. In lieu of it, varying substitutes[1] are prescribed, such as either an offering of flowers with the hands formed into the kaccapa mudrā, or union with the worshipper's own wife. In the same way, in lieu of wine, the paśu should (if a Brāhmaṇa) take milk, (if a (Kṣattriya) ghee, (if a Vaiśya) honey, and (if a Śūdra) a liquor made from rice. Salt, ginger, sesamum, wheat, māshkalai (beans), and garlic are various substitutes for meat; and the white brinjal vegetable, red radish, masur (a kind of gram), red sesamum, and pāniphala (an aquatic plant), take the place of fish. Paddy, rice, wheat, and gram generally are mudrā.

The vīra, or rather he who is qualified (adhikāri) for vīrācāra—since the true vīra is its finished product—commences sādhana with the rājasika pañcatattva first stated, which are employed for the destruction of the sensual tendencies which they connote. For the worship

---

1. See as to these and *post*, the Kulacūdāmaṇī, and chap. i of Bhairavayāmala.

of Śakti the pañcatattvas are declared to be essential. This Tantra declares that such worship without their use is but the practice of evil magic.

Upon this passage the commentator Jaganmohana Tarkālaṁkāra observes as follows: Let us consider what most contributes to the fall of a man, making him forget his duty, sink into sin, and die an early death. First among these are wine and women, fish, meat and mudrā, and accessories. By these things men have lost their manhood. Śiva then desires to employ these very poisons in order to eradicate the poison in the human system. Poison is the antidote for poison. This is the right treatment for those who long for drink or lust for women. The physician must, however, be an experienced one. If there be a mistake as to the application, the patient is likely to die. Śiva has said that the way of kulācāra is as difficult as it is to walk on the edge of a sword or to hold a wild tiger. There is a secret argument in favour of the pañcatattva, and those tattvas so understood should be followed by all. None, however, but the initiate can grasp this argument, and therefore Śiva has directed that it should not be revealed before anybody and everybody. An initiate, when he sees a woman, will worship her as his own mother or goddess (Iṣṭadevatā), and bow before her. The Viṣṇu-Purāṇa says that by feeding your desires you cannot satisfy them. It is like pouring ghee on fire. Though this is true, an experienced spiritual teacher (guru) will know how, by the application of this poisonous medicine, to kill the poison of saṁsāra. Śiva has, however, prohibited the indiscriminate publication of this. The meaning of this passage would

---

1. Mahānirvāṇa-Tantra, Chapter v, verses 23, 24. (See also Kailāsa-Tantra, Pūrva Khanda, chap. xc), where reasons are given why the worship of Devī is fruitless without the five elements; and where also they are identified with the five prāṇas and the five mahāpretas.

therefore appear to be this: The object of Tantrika worship is brahmasāyujjya, or union with Brahman. If that is not attained, nothing is attained. And, with men's propensities as they are, this can only be attained through the special treatment prescribed by the Tantras. If this is not followed, then the sensual propensities are not eradicated, and the work for the desired end of Tantra is useless as magic which, worked by such a man, leads only to the injury of others. The other secret argument here referred to is that by which it is shown that the particular·may be raised to the universal life by the vehicle of those same passions. which, when flowing only in an outward and downward current, are the most powerful bonds to bind him to the former. The passage cited refers to the necessity for the spiritual direction of the Guru. To the want of such is accredited the abuses of the system. When the patient (śiṣya) and the disease are working together, there is poor hope for the former; but when the patient, the disease, and the physician (guru) are on one, and that the wrong side, then nothing can save him from a descent on that downward path which it is the object of the sādhaka to prevent. Verse 67 in Chapter I of Mahānirvāṇa-Tantra is here, in point.

Owing, however, to abuses, particularly as regards the tattva of madya and maithuna, this Tantra, according to the current version, prescribes in certain cases, limitations as regards their use. It prescribes[1] that when the Kaliyuga is in full strength, and in the case of householders (gṛhastha) whose minds are engrossed with worldly affairs, the "three sweets" (madhuratraya) are to be substituted for wine. Those who are of virtuous temperament, and whose minds are turned towards the Brahman, are permit-

---

1. Chapter VIII, verse 171.

ted to take five cups of wine. So also as regards maithuna, this Tantra states[1] that men in this Kali age are by their nature weak and disturbed by lust, and by reason of this do not recognize woman (śakti) to be the image of the Deity. It accordingly[2] ordains that when the Kaliyuga is in full sway, the fifth tattva shall only be accomplished with svīyāśakti, or the worshipper's own wife, and that union with a woman who is not married to the sādhaka in either Brāhma or Śaiva forms is forbidden. In the case of other śakti (parakīyā and sādhāraṇī) it prescribes,[3] in lieu of maithuna, meditation by the worshipper upon the lotus feet of the Devī, together with japa of his iṣṭamantra. This rule, however, the Commentator says, is not of universal application. Śiva has, in this Tantra, prohibited sādhana with the last tattva, with parakīyā, and sādhāraṇī śaktī,[4] in the case of men of ordinary weak intellect ruled by lust; but for those who have by sādhana conquered their passions and attained the state of a true vīra, or siddha, there is no prohibition as to the mode of latāsādhana.[5] This Tantra appears to be,[6] in fact, a protest against the misuse of the tattva, which had followed upon a relaxation of the original rules and conditions governing them. Without the pañcatattva in one form or another, the śaktipūja cannot be performed. The Mother of the Universe must be worshipped with these elements. By their use the universe (jagatbrahmāṇḍa) itself is used as the article of worship. Wine signifies the

---

1. Chapter VIII, verse 173.
2. Chapter VI, verse 14.
3. Chapter VIII, verse 174.
4. See Uttara, Guptasādhana, Nigamakalpadruma, and other Tantras and Tantrasāra, (p. 698 et. seq.).
5. See Mahānirvāṇa-Tantra, Bhakta edition, p. 345.
6. For I have not yet had the opportunity of comparing the current Bengali with the Nepalese text.

power (śakti) which produces all fiery elements; meat and fish all terrestrial and aquatic animals; mudrā all vegetable life; and maithuna the will (icchā), action (kriyā) and knowledge (jñāna) śaktī of the Supreme Prakṛti productive of that great pleasure[1] which accompanies the process of creation.[2] To the Mother is thus offered the restless life of Her universe.

The object of all sādhana is the stimulation of the sattvaguṇa. When by such sādhana this guṇa largely preponderates, the sāttvika sādhana suitable for men of a high type of divyabhāva is adopted. In this latter sādhana the names of the pañcatattva are used symbolically for operations of a purely mental and spiritual character. Thus, the Kaivalya,[3] says that "wine" is that intoxicating knowledge acquired by yoga of the Parabrahman, which renders the worshipper senseless as regards the external world. Meat (māṁsa) is not any fleshy thing, but the act whereby the sādhaka consigns all his acts to Me (Mām). Matsya (fish) is that sāttvika knowledge by which through the sense of "mineness"[4] the worshipper sympathizes with the pleasure and pain of all beings. Mudrā is the act of relinquishing all association with evil which results in bondage, and maithuna is the union of the Śakti Kuṇḍalinī with Śiva in the body of the worshipper. This, the

---

1. Śiva in the Matṛkābheda-Tantra (chap. ii) says: (Yadrūpaṁ paramānandam tannāsti bhuvanatraye).

2. Nigama-Tattvasāra (chap. iv). See chap. xv of the Hara-Tattvadīdhīti; Mahānirvāṇa-Tantra, chap. v, verses 23, 24, and Kāmākhyā-Tantra. The Kailāsa-Tantra Purva-Khanda (chap. xc) identifies the pentad (pañcatattva) with the vital airs (prāṇādi) and the five mahāpretas (*vide post and ante*).

3. See p. 85 of Pañcatattvavīcāra, by Nilamani Mukhyopadhyāya.

4. A play upon the word matsya (fish).

Yoginī-Tantra says,[1] is the best of all unions for those who have already controlled their passions (yati). According to the Āgama-sāra, wine is the somadhārā, or lunar ambrosia, which drops from the brahmarandhra; Māṁsa (meat) is the tongue (mā), of which its part (aṁsa) is speech. The sādhaka, in "eating" it, controls his speech. Matsya (fish) are those two which are constantly moving in the two rivers Idā and Pingalā.[2] He who controls his breath by prāṇāyāma (*q.v.*), "eats" them by kumbhaka.[3] Mudrā is the awakening of knowledge in the pericarp of the great Sahasrāra Lotus, where the Ātmā, like mercury, resplendent as ten million suns, and deliciously cool as ten million moons, is united with the Devī Kuṇdalinī. The esoteric meaning of maithuna is thus stated by the Āgama: The ruddy-hued letter Ra is in the kuṇḍa,[4] and the letter Ma,[5] in the shape of bindu, is in the mahāyoni.[6] When Makāra (m), seated on the Haṁsa in the form of Akāra (a), unites with rakāra (r), then the Brahmajñāna, which is the source of supreme Bliss, is gained by the sādhaka, who is then called ātmārāma, for his enjoyment is in the Ātmā in the

---

1. Yoginī-Tantra (chap. v):

   Sahasrāropari bindau kundalyā melanaṁ śive,
   Maithunaṁ paramaṁ dravyaṁ yatīnāṁ parikīrtitam,

2. The nādi, so called (*vide ante*).

3. Retention of breath in prāṇāyāma.

4. The Maṇipūra-Cakra (*vide ante*).

5. This letter, according to the Kāmadhenu-Tantra (chap. ii), has five corners, is of the colour of the autumnal moon, is sattva guṇa, and is kaivalyarūpa and prakṛtirūpi. The coloration of the letters is variously given in the Tantrās. See also Bhāskararāya's Commentary on the Lalitā citing the Sanatkumāra-Saṁhitā and Mātṛkāviveka.

6. That is (here) the lightning-like triangular lines in the Sahasrāra. Bindu is literally the dot which represents the nasal sound. As to its Tantrik sense (*vide ante*).

7. For this reason, too, the name of Rama, which word also means sexual enjoyment, is equivalent to the liberator Brahman (Ra-a-ma).

16

Sahasrāra. This is the union on the purely sāttvika plane, which corresponds on the rājasika plane to the union of Śiva and Śakti in the persons of their worshippers.

The union of Śiva and Śakti is described as a true yoga[1] from which, as the Yāmala says, arises that joy which is known as the Supreme Bliss.[2]

## CAKRAPŪJA

Worship with the pañcatattva generally takes place in an assembly called a cakra, which is composed of men (sādhaka) and women (śakti), or Bhairava and Bhairavī. The worshippers sit in a circle (cakra), men and women alternately, the śakti sitting on the left of the sādhaka. The Lord of the cakra (cakrasvāmin, or cakreśvara) sits with his Śakti in the centre, where the wine-jar and other articles used in the worship are kept. During the cakra all eat, drink, and worship together, there being no distinction of caste.[3] No paśu should, however, be introduced. There are various kinds of cakras, such as the Vīra, Rāja, Deva, Mahā—Cakras productive, it is said, of various fruits for the participators therein.[4] Chapter VI of the Mahānirvāṇa-Tantra deals with the pañcatattva, and Chapter VIII gives an account of the Bhairavī and Tattva (or Divya) cakras.[5] The latter is for worshippers of the Brahma-Mantra.

---

1. See Tantrasāra, 702;

   Śivaśaktisamāyogāh,
   Yoga eva na saṁśayah.

2. *Ibid.*, 703; Saṁyogājjāyate sukhyam paramānandalakṣaṇam:

3. *Vide ante.*

4. The Rudra-yāmala says:

   Rājacakra rājadaṁ syat,
   Mahācakre samṛddhidam,
   Devacakre ca saubhāgyaṁ,
   Vīracakraṁca mokṣadaṁ.

5. Verses 153, 202, et seq.

# YOGA

THIS word, derived from the root Yuj ("to join"), is in grammar saṁdhi, in logic avayavaśakti, or the power of the parts taken together, and in its most widely known and present sense the union of the jīva, or embodied spirit, with the Paramātmā, or Supreme Spirit,[1] and the practices by which this union may be attained. There is a natural yoga, in which all beings are, for it is only by virtue of this identity in fact that they exist. This position is common ground, though in practice too frequently overlooked. "Primus modus unionis est, quo Deus, ratione suæ immensitatis est in omnibus rebus per essentiam, præsentiam, et potentiam; per essentiam us dans omnibus esse; per præsentiam et omnia prospiciens; per potentiam ut de omnibus disponens."[2] The mystical theologician cited, however, proceeds to say: "sed hæc unio animæ cum Deo est generalis, communis omnibus et ordinis naturalis.....illa namque de qua loquimur est ordinis supernaturalis actualis et fructiva." It is of this special yoga, though not in reality more "supernatural" than the first, that we here deal. Yoga in its technical sense is the realization of this identity, which exists, though it is not known, by the destruction of the false appearance of separation. "There is no bond equal in strength to māyā, and

---

1. As the Sāradā-tilaka (chap. xxv) says: Aikyām-jivā manorāhur-yogaṁ yogavihāradāh.

2. Summa Theologiae Mysticae, tom. iii, p. 8.

no force greater to destroy that bond than yoga. There is no better friend than knowledge (jñāna), nor worse enemy than egoism (ahaṁkāra). As to learn the Śāstra one must learn the alphabet, so yoga is necessary for the acquirement of tattvajñāna (truth)."[1] The animal body is the result of action, and from the body flows action, the process being compared to the seesaw movement of a ghatiyantra, or water-lifter.[2] Through their actions beings continually go from birth to death. The complete attainment of the fruit of yoga is lasting and unchanging life in the noumenal world of the Absolute.

Yoga is variously named according to the methods employed, but the two main divisions are those of the haṭhayoga (or ghatasthayoga) and samādhi yoga, of which rājayoga is one of the forms. Hathayoga is commonly misunderstood, both in its definition and aim being frequently identified with exaggerated forms of self-mortification.

The Gheraṇḍa-Saṁhita well defines it to be "the means whereby the excellent rājayoga is attained." Actual union is not the result of Haṭhayoga alone, which is concerned with certain physical processes preparatory or auxiliary to the control of the mind, by which alone union may be directly attained. It is, however, not meant that all the processes of Haṭhayoga here or in the books described are necessary for the attainment of rājayoga. What is necessary must be determined according to the circumstances of each particular case. What is suited or necessary in one case may not do so for another. A peculiar feature of Tāntrika vīrācāra is the union of the sādhaka and his śakti in

1. Gheraṇḍa-Sāṁhitā (chap. v. *et seq.*).

2. In drawing water, bullocks are employed to lower and raise the vessel. Human action is compared to the bullocks who now raise, now lower, the vessel into the waters (of the Saṁsāra).

latāsādhana. This is a process which is expressly forbidden to Paśus by the same Tantras which prescribe it for the Vīra. The union of Śiva and Śaktī in the higher sādhana is different in form, being the union of the Kuṇḍalinī-Śakti of the Mūlādhāra with the Bindu which is upon the Sahasrāra. This process, called the piercing of the six cakras, is described later on in a separate paragraph. Though, however, all Haṭhayoga processes are not necessary, some, at least, are generally considered to be so. Thus, in the well-known aṣṭāṅgayoga (eight-limbed yoga), of which samādhi is the highest end, the physical conditions and processes known as āsana and prāṇāyāma (*vide post*) are prescribed.

This yoga prescribes five exterior (bahiraṅga) methods for the subjugation of the body—namely (1) Yama, forbearance or self-control, such as sexual continence, avoidance of harm to others (ahiṁsā), kindness, forgiveness, the doing of good without desire for reward, absence of covetousness, temperance, purity of mind and body, etc.[1] (2) Niyama, religious observances, charity, austerities, reading of the Śāstra and Īśvara Praṇidhāna, persevering devotion to the Lord.[2] (3) Āsana, seated positions or postures (*vide post*). (4) Prāṇāyāma, regulation of the breath. A yogī renders the vital airs equable, and consciously produces the state of respiration which is favourable for mental concentration, as others do it occasionally and unconsciously (*vide post*). (5) Pratyāhāra, restraint of the senses, which follow in the path of the other four processes which deal with subjugation of the body.

---

1. Yoga-Yāgnavalkya (chap. i), where as to food it is said: "32 mouthfuls for an householder, 16 for a forest recluse, and 8 for a muni (saint and sage)."

2. *Ibid.*

There are then three interior (yogānga) methods for the subjugation of the mind—namely (6) Dhāraṇā, attention, steadying of the mind, the fixing of the internal organ (citta) in the particular manner indicated in the works on yoga. (7) Dhyāna or the uniform continuous contemplation of the object of thought; and (8) that samādhi which is called savikalpasamādhi. Savikalpasamādhi is a deeper and more intense contemplation on the Self to the exclusion of all other objects, and constituting trance or ecstasy. This ecstasy is perfected to the stage of the removal of the slightest trace of the distinction of subject and object in nirvikalpasamādhi, in which there is complete union with the Paramātmā, or Divine Spirit. By vairāgya (dispassion), and keeping the mind in its unmodified state, yoga is attained. This knowledge, Ahaṁ Brahmāsmi ("I am the Brahman"), does not produce liberation (mokṣa), but is liberation itself. Whether yoga is spoken of as the union of Kulakuṇḍalini with Paramaśiva, or the union of the individual soul (jīvātmā) with the Supreme Soul (paramātmā), or as the state of mind in which all outward thought is suppressed, or as the controlling or suppression of the thinking faculty (cittavṛtti), or as the union of the moon and the sun (Idā and Pingalā), Prāṇa and Apāna, Nāda and Bindu, the meaning and the end are in each case the same.

Yoga, in seeking mental control and concentration, makes use of certain preliminary physical processes (sādhana) such as the ṣaṭkarma, āsana, mudrā, and prāṇāyāma. By these four processes and three mental acts, seven qualities, known as śodhana, dridhatā, sthiratā, dhairya, lāghava, pratyakṣa, nirliptatva[1] (*vide post*), are acquired.

---

1. Gheranda Saṁhitā, First Upadeśa.

## ŚODHANA: ṢATKARMA

The first, or cleansing, is effected by the six processes known as the ṣatkarma. Of these, the first is Dhauti, or washing, which is fourfold, or inward washing (antar-dhauti), cleansing of the teeth, (dantadhauti), etc., of the "heart" (hṛddhauti), and of the rectum (mūladhauti). Antardhauti is also fourfold—namely, vātasāra, by which air is drawn into the belly and then expelled; vārisāra, by which the body is filled with water, which is then evacuated by the anus; vahnisāra, in which the nābhi-granthi is made to touch the spinal column (meru); and bahiṣkṛta, in which the belly is by kākinī-mudra[1] filled with air, which is retained half a yāma[2] and then sent downward. Dantadhauti is fourfold, consisting in the cleansing of the root of the teeth and tongue, the ears and the "hollow of the forehead" (kapāla-randhra). By hṛddhauti phlegm and bile are removed. This is done by a stick (daṇḍa-dhauti) or cloth (vāso-dhauti) pushed into the throat, or swallowed, or by vomiting (vamana-dhauti). Mūladhauti is done to cleanse the exit of the apānavāyu either with the middle finger and water or the stalk of a turmeric plant.

Vasti, the second of the ṣatkarma, is twofold and, is either of the dry (śuṣka) or watery (jala) kind. In the second form the yogi sits in the utkatāsana[3] posture in water up to the navel, and the anus is contracted and expanded by aśvinī mudrā; or the same is done in the paścimottānāsana,[4] and the abdomen below the navel

---

1. Gheraṇḍa-Saṁhitā, Third Upadeśa (verse 86).

2. A yāma is three hours.

3. Gheraṇḍa-Saṁhitā, Second Upadeśa (verse 23). That is, squatting, resting on the toes, the heels off the ground, and buttocks resting on heels.

4. *Ibid.*, verse 20.

is gently moved. In neti the nostrils are cleansed with a piece of string. Laulikī is the whirling of the belly from side to side. In trāṭakā the yogi, without winking, gazes at some minute object until the tears start from his eyes. By this the "celestial vision" (divya-dṛṣhti) so often referred to in the Tāntrika-upāsanā is acquired. Kapālabhāti is a process for the removal of phlegm, and is three-fold— vāta-krama by inhalation and exhalation; vyūtkrama by water drawn through the nostrils and ejected through the mouth; and śītkrama the reverse process.

These are the various processes by which the body is cleansed and made pure for the yoga practice to follow.

## DṚDHATĀ: ĀSANA

Dṛdhatā, or strength or firmness, the acquisition of which is the second of the above-mentioned processes, is attained by āsana.

Āsanas are postures of the body. The term is generally described as modes of seating the body. But the posture is not necessarily a sitting one; for some āsanas are done on the belly, back, hands, etc. It is said[1] that the āsanas are as numerous as living beings, and that there are 8,400,000 of these; 1,600 are declared to be excellent, and out of these thirty-two are auspicious for men, which are described in detail. Two of the commonest of these are muktapadmāsana[2] ("the loosened lotus seat"), the ordinary position for

1. Gheranda-Saṁhitā, Second Upadeśa. In the Śiva-Saṁhitā (chap. iii, verses 84-91) eighty-four postures are mentioned, of which four are recommended—viz., siddhāsana, ugrāsana, svastikāsana, and padmāsana.

2. The right foot is placed on the left thigh, the left foot on the right thigh and the hands are crossed and placed similarly on the thighs; the chin is placed on the breast, and the gaze fixed on the tip of the nose (see also Śiva-Sāṁhītā, chap. i, verse 52).

worship, and baddhapadmāsana.[1] Patañjali, on the subject of āsana, merely points out what are good conditions, leaving each one to settle the details for himself according to his own requirements. There are certain other āsanas, which are peculiar to the Tantras, such as muṇḍāsana, citāsana, and śavāsana, in which skulls, the funeral pyre, and a corpse respectively form the seat of the sādhaka. These, though they may have other ritual objects, form part of the discipline for the conquest of fear and the attainment of indifference, which is the quality of a yogī. And so the Tantras prescribe as the scene of such rites the solitary mountain-top, the lonely empty house and river-side, and the cremation-ground. The interior cremation-ground is there where the kāmik body and its passions are consumed in the fire of knowledge.

## STHIRATĀ: MUDRĀS

Sthiratā, or fortitude, is acquired by the practice of the mudrās. The mudrās dealt with in works of haṭhayoga are positions of the body. They are gymnastic, health-giving, and destructive of disease, and of death,[2] such as the jalādhara[3] and other mudrās. They also preserve from injury by fire, water, or air. Bodily action and the health resulting therefrom react upon the mind, and by the union of a perfect mind and body siddhi is by their means attained. The Gheraṇḍa-Saṁhitā describes a number of mudrās, of which those of importance may be selected. In the celebrat-

1. The same except that the hands are passed behind the back and the right hand holds the right toe, and the left hand the left toe. By this, increased pressure is placed on the mūlādhāra, and the nerves are braced with the tightening of the body.

2. Gheraṇḍa-Saṁhitā, Third Upadeśa.

3. *Ibid,* verse 12.

ed yonimudrā the yogī in siddhāsana stops with his fingers the ears, eyes, nostrils, and mouth. He inhales prāṇavāyu by kākinī-mudrā, and unites it with apānavāyu. Meditating in their order upon the six cakras, he arouses the sleeping Kulakuṇḍalinī by the mantra "Hūṁ Haṁsah," and raises Her to the Sahasrāra; then, deeming himself pervaded with the Śakti, and in blissful union (saṁgama) with Śiva, he meditates upon himself, as by reason of that union Bliss itself and the Brahman.[1] Aśvinīmudrā consists of the repeated contraction and expansion of the anus for the purpose of śodhana or of contraction to restrain the apāna in ṣatcakrabheda. Śakticālana employs the latter mudrā, which is repeated until vāyu manifests in the suṣuṁnā. The process is accompanied by inhalation and the union of prāna, and apāna whilst in siddhāsana.[2]

## DHAIRYA: PRATYĀHĀRA

Dhairya, or steadiness, is produced by pratyāhāra. Pratyāhāra, is the restraint of the senses, the freeing of the mind from all distractions, and the keeping of it under the control of the Ātmā. The mind is withdrawn from whatsoever direction it may tend by the dominant and directing Self. Pratyāhāra destroys the six sins.[3]

## LĀGHAVA: PRĀNĀYĀMA

From prānāyāma (*q.v.*) arises lāghava (lightness).

---

1. Gheraṇḍa-Saṁhitā, Third Upadeśa.

2. *Ibid.*, verses 37, 49, 82.

3. *Ibid.*, Fourth Upadeśa. The Sāradātilaka defines pratyāhāra as indriyāṇāṁ vicaratāṁ viṣayeṣu balādaharaṇam tebhyah pratyāhāro vidhiyate (pratyāhāra is known as the forcible abstraction of the senses wandering over their objects).

All beings say the ajapā-Gāyatrī, which is the expulsion of the breath by Haṁkāra, and its inspiration by Sahkāra, 21,600 times a day. Ordinarily, the breath goes forth a distance of 12 fingers' breadth, but in singing, eating, walking, sleeping, coition, the distances are 16, 20, 24, 30, and 36 breadths respectively. In violent exercise these distances are exceeded, the greatest distance being 96 breadths. Where the breathing is under the normal distance, life is prolonged. Where it is above that, it is shortened. Pūraka is inspiration, and recaka expiration. Kumbhaka is the retention of the breath between these two movements. Kumbhaka is, according to the Gheraṇḍa-Saṁhita, of eight kinds: sahita, sūryabheda, ujjāyī, śītali, bhastrikā, bhārmarī, mūrchchha, and kevalī. Prāṇāyāma similarly varies. Prāṇāyāma is the control of the breath and other vital airs. It awakens śakti, frees from disease, produces detachment from the world, and bliss. It is of varying values, being the best (uttama) where the measure is 20; middling (madhyama) when at 16 it produces spinal tremour; and inferior (adhama) when at 12 it induces perspiration. It is necessary that the nādī should be cleansed, for air does not enter those which are impure. The cleansing of the nādī (nādī-śuddhi) is either samanu or nirmanu—that is, with or without, the use of bīja. According to the first form, the yogī in padmāsana does gurunyāsa according to the directions of the guru. Meditating on "yaṁ," he does japa through Idā of the bīja 16 times, kumbhaka with japa of bīja 64 times, and then exhalation through the solar nādī and japa of bīja 32 times. Fire is raised from maṇipūra and united with pṛthivī. Then follows inhalation by the solar nādī with the vahni bīja, 16 times, kuṁbhaka with 64 japa of the bīja, followed by exhalation through the lunar nādī and japa of the bīja 32 times. He then meditates on the lunar brilliance gazing at the tip of the nose, and inhales by Idā with japa of the bīja "thaṁ" 16 times. Kuṁbhaka is done with the bīja vaṁ 64 times. He then thinks of himself as flooded by nectar, and considers that the nādīs have been washed. He exhales by Pingalā with 32 japa of the bīja laṁ, and considers himself thereby as strengthened. He then takes his seat on a mat of kuśa-grass, a deerskin, etc., and, facing east or north, does prānāyāma. For its exercise there must be, in addition to nādī śuddhi, consideration of proper place, time, and food. Thus, the place should not be so distant as to induce anxiety, nor in an unprotected place, such as a forest, nor in a city or crowded locality, which induces distraction. The food should be pure, and of a vegetarian character. It should not be too hot or too cold, pungent, sour, salt, or bitter. Fasting, the taking of one meal a day, and the like, are prohibited. On the contrary, the Yogī should not remain without food for more than one yāma (three hours). The food taken should be light and strengthening. Long walks and other violent exercises should be avoided, as also—certainly in the case of beginners—sexual intercourse. The stomach should only be half filled. Yoga should be commenced, it is said, in spring or autumn. As stated, the forms of prāṇāyāma vary. Thus, sahita, which is either with (sagarbha) or without (nirgarbha) bīja, is, according to the former form, as follows: The sādhaka meditates on Vidhi (Brahmā), who is full of rajo-guṇa, red in colour, and the image of akāra. He inhales by Idā in six measures (mātrā). Before kuṁbhaka he does the uddīyāṇabhandha mudrā. Meditating on Hari (Viśnu) as sattvamaya and the black bīja ukāra, he does kuṁbhaka with 64 japa of the bīja; then, meditating on Śiva as tamomaya and his white bīja makāra, he exhales through Pingalā with 32 japa of the bīja; then, inhaling by

Piṅgalā, he does kuṁbhaka, and exhales by Idā with the same bīja. The process is repeated in the normal and reversed order.

## PRATYAKṢA : DHYĀNA

Through dhyāna is gained the third quality of realization or pratyakṣa. Dhyāna, or meditation, is of three kinds: (1) sthūla, or gross; (2) jyotih; (3) sūkṣma, or subtle.[1] In the first the form of the Devatā is brought before the mind. One form of dhyāna for this purpose is as follows: Let the sādhaka think of the great ocean of nectar in his heart. In the middle of that ocean is the island of gems, the shores of which are made of powdered gems. The island is clothed with a kadamba forest in yellow blossom. This forest is surrounded by Mālati, Caṁpaka, Pārijāta, and other fragrant trees. In the midst of the Kadamba forest there rises the beautiful Kalpa tree, laden with fresh blossom and fruit. Amidst its leaves the black bees hum and the koel birds make love. Its four branches are the four Vedas. Under the tree there is a great mandapa of precious stones, and within it a beautiful bed, on which let him picture to himself his Iṣtadevatā. The Guru will direct him as to the form, raiment, vāhana, and the title of the Devatā. Jyotirdhyāna is the infusion of fire and life (tejas) into the form so imagined. In the mūlādhāra lies the snake-like Kuṇḍalinī. There the jīvātmā, as it were the tapering flame of a candle, dwells. The Sādhaka then meditates

---

1. Gheraṇḍa-Saṁhitā, Sixth Upadeśa. It is said by Bhāskararāya, in the Lalitā (verse 2), that there are three forms of the Devī which equally partake of both the prakāśa and vimarśa aspects—viz., the physical (sthūla), the subtle (sūkṣma) and the supreme (para). The physical form has hands, feet, etc., the subtle consists of mantra, and the supreme is the vāsanā or, in the technical sense of the Mantra śāstrā, real or own.

upon the tejomaya Brahman, or, alternatively, between the eyebrows on praṇavātmaka, the flame emitting its lustre.

Sūkṣma-dhyāna is meditation on Kuṇḍalinī with śāmbhavī-mudrā after She has been roused. By this yoga (*vide post*) the ātmā is revealed (ātma-sākṣātkāra).

## NIRLIPTATVA: SAMĀDHI

Lastly, through samādhi the quality of nirliptatva, or detachment, and thereafter mukti (liberation) is attained. Samādhi considered as a process is intense mental concentration, with freedom from all saṁkalpa, and attachment to the world, and all sense of "mineness," or self-interest (mamatā). Considered as the result of such process it is the union of Jīva with the Paramātmā.[1]

## FORMS OF SAMĀDHI-YOGA

This samādhi yoga is, according to the Gheraṇda-Saṁhitā, of six kinds:[2] (1) Dhyāna-yoga-samādhi, attained by śāṁbhavī-mudrā,[3] in which, after meditation on the Bindu-Brahman and realization of the Atmā (ātmapratyakṣa), the latter is resolved into the Mahākāśa. (2) Nāda-yoga, attained by khecarī-mudrā,[4] in which the fraenum of the tongue is cut, and the latter is lengthened until it reaches the space between the eyebrows, and is then introduced in a reversed position into the mouth. (3) Rasānandayoga, attained by kuṁbhaka,[5] in which the sādhaka in a silent place closes both ears and does pūraka and kuṁbhaka until he hears the word nāda in sounds varying in strength from that of

1. See Commentary on verse 51 of the ṣatcakranirūpaṇa.
2. Seventh Upadeśa.
3. *Ibid.*, Third Upadeśa (verses 65 *et. seq.*).
4. *Ibid.*, verses 25 *et seq.*
5. *Ibid.*, Fifth Upadeśa (verses 77 *et seq.*).

the cricket's chirp to that of the large kettle-drum. By daily practice the anāhata sound is heard, and the jyoti with the manas therein is seen, which is ultimately dissolved in the supreme Viṣṇu. (4) Laya-siddhi-yoga, accomplished by the celebrated yonimudrā already described.[1] The sādhaka, thinking of himself as Śakti and the Paramātmā as Puruṣa, feels himself in union (saṁgama) with Siva, and enjoys with him the bliss which is śṛngārarasa,[2] and becomes Bliss itself, or the Brahman. (5) Bhakti-Yoga, in which meditation is made on the Iṣtadevatā with devotion (bhakti) until, with tears flowing from the excess of bliss, the ecstatic condition is attained. (6) Rājayoga, accomplished by aid of the manomurcchā kuṁbhaka.[3] Here the manas detached from all worldly objects is fixed between the eyebrows in the ājñācakra, and kuṁbhaka is done. By the union of the manas with the ātma, in which the jñāni sees all things, rāja-yoga-samādhi is attained.

## ṢATCAKRA—BHEDA

The piercing of the six cakras is one of the most important subjects dealt with in the Tantra, and is part of the practical yoga process of which they treat. Details of practice[4] can only be learnt from a Guru, but generally

---

1. In the Lalitā (verse 142) the Devī is addressed as Layakarī—the cause of laya or mental absorption.

2. Śṛngāra is the love sentiment or sexual passion and sexual union. The first of the eight or nine rasa (sentiments)—viz., śṛngāra, vīra (heroism), karuṇa (compassion), adbhutā (wondering), hāsya (humour), bhayānaka (fear), bibhatsa (disgust), raudra (wrath) to which Maṇmathabhatta, author of the Kāvyaprakāśa adds śānti (peace).

3. *Ibid.*, Fifth Upadeśa, verse 82.

4. Fuller details are given in the Author's translation from the Sanskrit of the ṣatcakranirūpana by Pūrnānanda Svāmi, author of the celebrated Śāktānandatarangini.

it may be said that the particular is raised to the universal life, which as cit is realizable only in the sahasrāra in the following manner: The jīvātmā in the subtle body, the receptacle of the five vital airs (pañca-prāṇa), mind in its three aspects of manas, ahaṁkāra, and buddhi, the five organs of action (pancakarmendriyas) and the five organs of perception (pancajñānendriyas) is united with the Kulakuṇḍalinī. The Kandarpa or Kāma Vāyu in the mūlādhāra, a form of the Apāna-Vāyu, is given a leftward revolution and the fire which is round Kuṇḍaliṇī is kindled. By the bīja "Hūṁ," and the heat of the fire thus kindled, the coiled and sleeping Kuṇḍalinī is awakened. She who lay asleep around svayambhu-linga, with her coils three circles and a half closing the entrance of the brahmadvāra, will, on being roused, enter that door and move upwards, united with the jīvātmā.

On this upward movement, Brahmā, Sāvitrī, Dākinī-Śakti, the Devās, bīja, and vritti, are dissolved in the body of Kuṇḍalinī. The Mahī-maṇdala or pṛthivī is converted into the bīja "Laṁ," and is also merged in Her body. When Kuṇḍalinī leaves the mūlādhāra, that lotus which, on the awakening of Kuṇḍalinī had opened and turned its flower upwards, again closes and hangs downward. As Kuṇḍalinī reaches the svādhiṣthāna-cakra, that lotus opens out, and lifts its flowers upwards. Upon the entrance of Kuṇḍalinī, Mahāviṣṇu, Mahālakṣmī, Sarasvatī, Rākinī Śakti, Deva, Mātṛās, and vritti, Vaikuṇthadhāmā, Golaka, and the Deva and Devī residing therein are dissolved in the body of Kuṇḍalinī. The pṛthivī, or "earth" bīja "Laṁ" is dissolved in apas, and apas converted into the bīja vaṁ remains in the body of Kuṇḍalinī. When the Devi reaches the maṇi-pūra cakra all that is in the cakra merges in Her body. The Varuṇa bīja "vaṁ" is dissolved in fire, which remains in the body of the Devī as the Bīja "raṁ." The cakra is called the Brahma-granthi (or knot of Brahma). The piercing of this cakra may involve considerable pain, physical disorder, and even disease. On this account the directions of an experienced Guru are necessary, and therefore also other modes of yoga have been recommended for those to whom they are applicable: for in such modes, activity is provoked directly in the higher centre and it is not necessary that the lower cakra should be pierced. Kuṇḍalinī next reaches the anāhata-cakra, where all which is therein is merged in Her. The bīja of Tejas, "raṁ," disappears in Vāyu and Vāyu converted into its bīja "Yaṁ" merges in the body of Kuṇḍalinī. This cakra is known as Viṣnu-granthi (knot of Viṣnu). Kuṇḍalinī then ascends to the abode of Bhārati (or Sarasvati) or the viśuddha-cakra. Upon Her entrance, Arddha-nārīśvara Śiva, Śākinī, the sixteen vowels, mantra, etc., are dissolved in the body of Kuṇḍalinī. The bīja of Vāyu, "yaṁ," is dissolved in ākāśa, which itself being transformed into the bīja "haṁ," is merged in the body of Kuṇḍalinī. Piercing the lalanā-cakra, the Devī reaches the ājñācakra, where Parama-Śiva, Siddha-Kālī, the Deva, guṇas, and all else therein, are absorbed into Her body. The bīja of akāśa, "Haṁ," is merged in the manas-cakra, and mind itself in the body of Kuṇḍalinī. The ājñācakra is known as Rudra-granthī (or knot of Rudra or Śiva). After this cakra has been pierced, Kuṇḍalinī of Her own motion ùnites with Parama-Siva. As She proceeds upwards from the two-petalled lotus, the nirālaṁba-puri, praṇava, nāda, etc., are merged in Her.

The Kuṇḍalinī has then in her progress upwards absorbed in herself the twenty-four tattvās commencing with the gross elements, and then unites Herself and becomes one with Parama-Śiva. This is the maithuna (coition) of the sāttvika-pañca-tattvas. The nectar[1] which flows from such union floods the kṣudrabrahmāṇda or human body. It is then that the sādhaka, forgetful of all in this world, is immersed in ineffable bliss.

Thereafter the sādhaka, thinking of the vāyu-bīja "yaṁ" as being in the left nostril, inhales through Idā, making japa of the bīja sixteen times. Then, closing both nostrils, he makes japa of the bīja sixty-four times. He then thinks that black "man of sin"[2] (Pāpapuruṣa) in the left cavity of the abdomen is being dried up (by air), and so thinking he exhales through the right nostril Pingalā, making japa of the bīja thirty-two times. The sādhaka then meditating upon the red-coloured bīja "raṁ" in the maṇipūra, inhales, making sixteen japas of the bīja, and then closes the nostrils, making sixteen japas. While making the japa he thinks that the body of "the man of sin" is being burnt and reduced to ashes (by fire). He then exhales through the right nostril with thirty-two japas. He then meditates upon the white candra-bīja "thaṁ." He next inhales through Ida, making japa of the bīja sixteen times, closes both nostrils with japa done sixty-four times, and exhales through Pingalā with thirty-two japas. During inhalation, holding of breath, and exhalation, he should consider that a new celestial body is being formed by the nectar (composed of all the letters of the alphabet, mātṛkā-varṇa) dropping from the moon. In a similar way with the bīja "vaṁ," the formation of the body is continued, and with the bīja "laṁ"

---

1. In the Cintāmaṇistava attributed to Śri Śaṁkarācārya it is said: "This family woman (kuṇḍalinī), entering the royal road (suṣumnā), taking rest at intervals in the secret places (cakra), embraces the Supreme Spouse and makes the nectar to flow (in the sahasrāra.)"

2. As to Pāpa-puruṣa see Mahānirvāṇa-Tantra Ullāsa, V. (verses 98, 99).

it is completed and strengthened. Lastly, with the mantra "Sōhaṁ," the sādhaka leads the jīvātmā into the heart. Thus Kuṇḍalinī, who has enjoyed Her union with Parama-śiva, sets out on her return journey the way she came. As she passes through each of the cakras all that she has absorbed therefrom come out from herself and take their several places in the cakra.

In this manner she again reaches the mūlādhāra, when all that is described to be in the cakras are in the position which they occupied before her awakening.

The Guru's instructions are to go above the ājñā-cakra, but no special directions are given; for after this cakra has been pierced the sādhaka can reach the brahmasthāna unaided. Below the "seventh month of Śiva" the relationship of Guru and śiṣya ceases. The instructions of the seventh āmnāya is not expressed (aprakāśita).

## SIN AND VIRTUE

According to Christian conceptions,[1] sin is a violation of the personal will of, and apostasy from, God. The flesh is the source of lusts which oppose God's commands, and in this lies its positive significance for the origin of a bias of life against God. According to St. Thomas, in the original state, no longer held as the normal, the lower powers were subordinate to reason, and reason subject to God. "Original sin" is formally a "defect of original righteousness," and materially "concupiscence." As St. Paul says (Rom. vii. 8, 14), the pneumatic law, which declares war on the lusts, meets with opposition from the "law in the members." These and similar notions involve a religious and moral conscious judgment which is assumed to exist in humanity alone. Hindu notions of pāpa (wrong) and puṇya (that which is pure, holy, and right) have a wider content. The latter is accordance and working with the will of Iśvara (of whom the jīva is itself the embodiment), as manifested at any particular time in the general direction taken by the cosmic process, as the former is the contrary. The two terms are relative to the state of evolution and the surrounding circumstances of the jīva to which they are applied. Thus, the impulse towards individuality which is necessary and just on the path of inclination or "going forth" (pravṛtti-mārga), is wrongful as a hindrance to the attainment of unity, which is the goal of the path of return (nivṛtti-mārga) where inclinations should cease. In short, what makes for progress on the one path is a hindrance on the

1. See authorities cited in Schaaff Herzog Dict.

other. The matter, when rightly understood, is not (except, perhaps, sometimes popularly) viewed from the juristic standpoint of an external Lawgiver, His commands, and those subject to it, but from that in which the exemplification of the moral law is regarded as the true and proper expression of the jīva's own evolution. Morality, it has been said, is the true nature of a being. For the same reason wrong is its destruction. What the jīva actually does is the result of his karma. Further, the term jīva, though commonly applicable to the human embodiment of the ātmā, is not limited to it. Both pāpa and puṇya may therefore be manifested in beings of a lower rank than that of humanity in so far as what they (whether consciously or unconsciously) do is a hindrance to their true development. Thus, in the Yoga-Vāsiṣtha it is said that even a creeping plant acquired merit by association with the holy muni on whose dwelling it grew. Objectively considered, sin is concisely defined as duḥkhajanakaṁ pāpam. It is that which has been, is, and will be the cause of pain, mental or physical, in past, present and future births. The pain as the consequence of the action done need not be immediate. Though, however, the suffering may be experienced as a result later than the action of which it is the cause, the consequence of the action is not really something separate, but a part of the action itself—namely, the part of it which belongs to the future. The six chief sins are kāma, krodha, lobha, moha, mada, mātsarya—lust, anger, covetousness, ignorance or delusion, pride and envy.[1] All wrong is at base self-seeking, in ignorance or disregard of the unity of the Self in all creatures. Virtue (puṇya), therefore, as

1. This in part corresponds with the Christian classification of the "seven deadly sins": pride, coveteousness, lust, anger, envy, gluttony, and sloth which is deliberately persisted in, drive from the soul all state of grace.

the contrary of sin, is that which is the cause of happiness (sukhajanakaṁ pūṇyam). That happiness is produced either in this or future births, or leads to the enjoyment of heaven (Svarga). Virtue is that which leads towards the unity whose substance is Bliss (ānanda). This good karma produces pleasant fruit, which, like all the results of karma, is transitory. As Śruti says: "It is not by acts or the pindas offered by one's children or by wealth, but by renunciation that men have attained liberation."[1] It is only by escape through knowledge, that the jīva becoming one with the unchanging Absolute attains lasting rest. It is obvious that for those who obtain such release neither vice nor virtue, which are categories of phenomenal being, exist.

## KARMA

Karma is action, its cause, and effect. There is no uncaused action, nor action without effect. The past, the present, and the future are linked together as one whole. The icchā, jñāna, and kriyā śaktis manifest in the jīvātmā living on the worldly plane as desire, knowledge, and action. As the Bṛhadāraṇyaka-Upaniṣad says: "Man is verily formed of desire. As is his desire, so is his thought. As is his thought, so is his action. As is his action, so his attainment."[2] These fashion the individual's karma. "He who desires goes by work to the

---

1. Na karmaṇā, na prajayā, dhanena

Tyāgena eke amṛtatvaṁ ānaśuh. (Taittiriyopaniṣad).

2. Chapter IV, iv. 5.

object on which his mind is set."[1] "As he thinks, so he becometh,"[2] Then, as to action, "whatsoever a man sows that shall he reap." The matter is not one of punishment and reward, but of consequence, and the consequence of action is but a part of it. If anything is caused, its result is caused, the result being part of the original action, which continues, and is transformed into the result. The jīvātmā experiences happiness for his good acts and misery for his evil ones.[3]

Karma is of three kinds—viz., saṁcita-karma—that is, the whole vast accumulated mass of the unexhausted karma of the past, whether good or bad, which has still to be worked out. This past karma is the cause of the character of the succeeding births, and, as such, is called saṁskāra, or vāsanā. The second form of karma is prārabdha, or that part of the first which is ripe, and which is worked out and bears fruit in the present birth. The third is the new karma, which man is continually making by his present and future actions, and is called vartamāna and āgāmī.[4] The embodied soul (jīvātmā), whilst in the saṁsāra or phenomenal world, is by its nature ever making present karma and experiencing the past. Even the Devas themselves are subject to time and karma.[5] By his karma a jīva may become an Indra.[6]

---

1. Chapter IV, iv. 6.
2. Chāndogya Upaniṣad, III, xiv. i.
3. Mahābhārata, Śānti-Parva, cci. 23, ccxi. 12.
4. Devī-Bhāgavata. VI. x, 9, 12, 13, 14.
5. So it is said:

   Namastat karmabhyo vidhirapi na yebhyah prabhavati, and
   Ye samastajagatṣriṣtisthitisaṁhārakarenāh.
   Tepi kāleṣu līyante kālo hi balavattaraḣ.
6. Devī Bhāgavata IX, xxvii, 18-20.

Karma is thus the invisible (adṛṣṭa), the product of ordained or prohibited actions capable of giving bodies. It is either good or bad, and altogether these are called the impurity of action (karma-mala). Even good action, when done with a view to its fruits, can never secure liberation. Those who think of the reward will receive benefit in the shape of that reward. Liberation is the work of Śiva-Śakti, and is gained only by brahmajñāna, the destruction of the will to separate life, and realization of unity with the Supreme. All accompanying action must be without thought of self. With the cessation of desire the tie which binds man to the saṁsāra is broken. According to the Tantra, the sādhana and ācāra (*q. v.*) appropriate to an individual depends upon his karma. A man's tendencies, character, and temperament is moulded by his saṁcita karma. As regards prārabdha-karma, is it unavoidable. Nothing can be done but to work it out. Some systems prescribe the same method for men of diverse tendencies. But the Tantra recognizes the force of karma, and moulds its methods to the temperament produced by it. The needs of each vary, as also the methods which will be the best suited to each to lead them to the common goal. Thus, forms of worship which are permissible to the vīra are forbidden to the paśu. The guru must determine that for which the sādhaka is qualified (adhikārī).

# FOUR AIMS OF BEING

THERE is but one thing which all seek—happiness—though it be of differing kinds and sought in different ways. All forms, whether sensual, intellectual, or spiritual, are from the Brahman, who is Itself the Source and Essence of all Bliss, and Bliss itself (ras ovai sah). Though issuing from the same source--pleasure differs in its forms in being higher and lower, transitory or durable, or permanent. Those on the path of desire (pravṛtti-mārga) seek it through the enjoyments of this world (bhukti) or in the more durable, though still impermanent delights of heaven (svarga). He who is on the path of return (nivṛtti-mārga) seeks happiness, not in the created worlds, but in everlasting union with their primal source (mukti); and thus it is said that man can never be truly happy until he seeks shelter with Brahman, which is Itself the great Bliss (rasam hi vāyam labdhvā ānandī bhavati).

The eternal rhythm of the Divine Breath is outwards from spirit to matter and inwards from matter to spirit. Devī as Māyā evolves the world. As Mahā-māyā She recalls it to Herself. The path of outgoing is the way of pravṛtti; that of return nivṛtti. Each of these movements is divine. Enjoyment (bhukti) and liberation (mukti) are each Her gifts.[1] And in the third chapter of the work cited it is said that of Viṣṇu and Śiva mukti only can be

1. As also Svargā (see Śāktānanda-taranginị, chap. i).

had, but of Devī both bhukti and mukti; and this is so in so far as the Devī is, in a peculiar sense, the source whence those material things come from which enjoyment (bhoga) arises. All jīvas on their way to humanity,[1] and the bulk of humanity itself, are on the forward path, and rightly seeks the enjoyment which is appropriate to its stage of evolution.

The thirst for life will continue to manifest itself until the point of return is reached and the outgoing energy is exhausted. Man, must, until such time, remain on the path of desire. In the hands of Devī is the noose of desire. Devī herself is both desire[2] and that light of knowledge which in the wise who have known enjoyment lays bare its futilities. But one cannot renounce until one has enjoyed, and so of the world-process itself it is said: that the unborn ones, the Puruṣas, are both subservient to Her (prakṛti), and leave Her by reason of viveka.[3]

Provision is made for the worldly life which is the "outgoing" of the Supreme. And so it is said that the Tāntrika has both enjoyment (bhukti) and liberation (mukti).[4] But enjoyment itself is not without its law. Desire is not to be let loose without bridle.[5] The mental

---

1. Including, according to a caustic observer, the large number of men who may be more properly described as candidates for humanity.

2. See Caṇḍī, Devī is manifested in desire, etc.

3. And so Śruti (Taittirīya-Āranyaka) says:

Ajāmekāṁ lohit-śukla kṛṣṇāṁ,
Bahvīṁ prajām janayantiṁ śarūpāṁ,
Ajo hyeko jūṣamāno' nuśete
Jahātyenāṁ bhukta-bhogāmajonyah:

and see Saṁkhya Tattva-Kaumudi.

4. See Chapter IV, verse 39 post, and Chapter I, verse 51, where the Tantra are described as the givers of both bhukti and mukti. See notes to same as to bhoga.

5. As to svecchā, see notes to Chapter III, verse 96 post.

self is, as is commonly said, the charioteer of the body, of which the senses are the horses. Contrary to mistaken notions on the subject, the Tantras take no exception to the ordinary rule that it is necessary not to let them run away. If one would not be swept away and lost in the mighty force which is the descent into matter, thought and action must be controlled by Dharma. Hence the first three of the aims of life (trivarga) on the path of pravṛtti are dharma, artha, and kāma.

## DHARMA

Dharma means that which is to be held fast or kept —law, usage, custom, religion, piety, right, equity, duty, good works, and morality. It is, in short, the eternal and immutable (sanātana) principles which hold together the universe in its parts and in its whole, whether organic or inorganic matter. "That which supports and holds together the peoples (of the universe) is dharma." "It was declared for well-being and bringeth well-being. It upholds and preserves. Because it supports and holds together, it is called Dharma. By Dharma are the people upheld." It is, in short, not an artifical rule, but the principle of right living. The mark of dharma and of the good is ācāra (good conduct), from which dharma is born and fair fame is acquired here and hereafter.[1] The sages embraced ācāra as the root of all tapas.[2] Dharma is not only the principle of right living, but also its application. That course of meritorious action by which man fits himself for this world, heaven, and liberation. Dharma is also the result of good action—that is, the merit acquired thereby. The basis of

---

1. Mahābhārata, Śānti-Parva (CIC. 88). Anuśāsana-Parva, CIV.
2. Manusmrti (I. 108, 110).

the sanātana-dharma is revelation (śruti) as presented in the various Śāstras.—Smṛti, Purāṇa, and Tantra. In the Devī-Bhāgavata[1] it is said that in the Kaliyuga Viṣṇu in the form of Vyāsa divides the one Veda into many parts, with the desire to benefit men, and with the knowledge that they are short-lived and of small intelligence, and hence unable to master the whole. This dharma is the first of the four leading aims (caturvarga) of all being.

## KĀMA

Kāma is desire, such as that for wealth, success, family, position, or other forms of happiness for self or others. It also involves the notion of the necessity for the possession of great and noble aims, desires, and ambitions, for such possession is the characteristic of greatness of soul. Desire, whether of the higher or lower kinds, must, however, be lawful, for man is subject to dharma, which regulates it.

## ARTHA

Artha (wealth) stands for the means by which this lite may be maintained—in the lower sense, food, drink, money, house, land, and other property; and in the higher sense the means by which effect may be given to the higher desires, such as that of worship, for which artha may be necessary, aid given to others, and so forth. In short, it is all the necessary means by which all right desire, whether of the lower or higher kinds, may be fulfilled. As the desire must be a right desire—for man is subject to dharma, which regulates them—so also must be the means sought, which are equally so governed.

---

1. I. iii. 99.

The first group is known as the trivarga, which must be cultivated whilst man is upon the pravritti mārga: Unless and until there is renunciation on entrance upon the path of return, where inclination ceases (nivṛtti-mārga), man must work for the ultimate goal by meritorious acts (dharma), desires (kāma), and by the lawful means (artha) whereby the lawful desires which give birth to righteous acts are realized. Whilst on the pravṛtti-mārga "the trivarga should be equally cultivated, for he who is addicted to one only is despicable" (dharmārthakāmāh samameva sevyāh yo hyekasaktah sa jano-jaganyah.)[1].

## MOKṢA

Of the four aims, mokṣa or mukti is the truly ultimate end, for the other three are ever haunted by the fear of Death, the Ender.[2]

Mukti means "loosening" or liberation. It is advisable to avoid the term "salvation," as also other Christian terms, which connote different, though in a loose sense, analogous ideas. According to the Christian doctrine (soteriology), faith in Christ's Gospel and in His Church effects salvation, which is the forgiveness of sins mediated by Christ's redeeming activity, saving from judgment, and admitting to the Kingdom of God. On the other hand, mukti means loosening from the bonds of the saṁsāra (phenomenal existence), resulting in a union (of various degrees of completeness) of the embodied spirit (jīvātmā)

---

1. As, for instance, a householder, who spends all his time in worship to the neglect of his family and worldly estate. The śāstra says, "either one thing or the other; when in the world be rightly of it; when adopting the specifically religious life, leave it"—a statement of the maxim "be thorough".

2. Viṣṇu-Bhāgavata, IV, xxii, 34, 35.

or individual life with the Supreme Spirit (paramātmā). Liberation can be attained by spiritual knowledge (ātmajñāna) alone, though it is obvious that such knowledge must be preceded by, and accompanied with, and, indeed, can only be attained in the sense of actual realization, by freedom from sin and right action through adherence to dharma. The idealistic system of Hinduism, which posits the ultimate reality as being in the nature of mind, rightly, in such cases, insists on what, for default of a better term, may be described as the intellectual, as opposed to the ethical, nature. Not that it fails to recognize the importance of the latter, but regards it as subsidiary and powerless of itself to achieve that extinction of the modifications of the energy of consciousness which constitutes the supreme mukti known as Kaivalya. Such extinction cannot be effected by conduct alone, for such conduct, whether good or evil, produces karma, which is the source of the modifications which it is man's final aim to suppress. Mokṣa belongs to the nivritti mārga, as the trivarga appertain to the pravṛtti-mārga.

There are various degrees of mukti, some more perfect than the others, and it is not, as is generally supposed one state.

There are four future states of Bliss, or pada, being in the nature of abodes—viz., sālokya, sāmīpya, sārūpya, and sāyujya—that is, living in the same loka, or region, with the Deva worshipped; being near the Deva; receiving the same form or possessing the same aiśvarya (Divine qualities) as the Deva, and becoming one with the Deva worshipped. The abode to which the jīva attains depends upon the worshipper and the nature of his worship, which may be with, or without, images, or of the Deva regarded as distinct from the worshipper and with attributes, and so forth. The four abodes are the result of action, transitory and conditioned. Mahānirvāṇa, or Kaivalya, the real mokṣa, is the result of spiritual knowledge (jñāna),[1] and is unconditioned and permanent. Those who know the Brahman, recognizing that the worlds resulting from action are imperfect, reject them, and attain to that unconditioned Bliss which transcends them all. Kaivalya is the supreme state of oneness without attributes, the state in which, as the Yoga-sutra says, modification of the energy of consciousness is extinct, and when it is established in its own real nature.[2]

Liberation is attainable while the body is yet living, in which case there exists a state of jīvanmukti celebrated in the Jīvanmukti-gītā of Dattātreya. The soul, it is true, is not really fettered, and any appearance to the contrary is illusory. There is, in fact, freedom, but though mokṣa is already in possession still, because of the illusion that it is not yet attained, means must be taken to remove the illusion, and the jīva who succeeds in this is jīvanmukta, though in the body, and is freed from future embodiments. The enlightened Kaula, according to the Nityanita, sees no difference between mud and sandal, friend and foe, a dwelling-house and the cremation-ground. He knows that the Brahman is all, that the Supreme soul (paramātmā) and the individual soul (jīvātmā) are one, and freed from all attachment he is jīvanmukta, or liberated, whilst yet living. The means whereby mukti is attained is the yoga process (*vide ante*).

---

1. That is which gives mokṣa, other forms being called vijñāna.
   Mokṣe dhir jñānam anayatra.
   vijñānaṁ śilpa-śāstrayoh. (Nāmalinganusā samakāṇḍa 1-4-6).
2. See Bhāskararāya's Commentary on Lalitā Sahasranāma, śloka, 125.

## SIDDHI

Siddhi is produced by sādhana. The former term, which literally means "success," includes accomplishment, achievement, success, and fruition of all kinds. A person may thus gain siddhi in speech, siddhi in mantra, etc. A person is siddha also who has perfected his spiritual development. The various powers attainable—namely, aṇimā, mahimā, laghimā, garimā, prapti, prākāmyā, īśitva, vaśitva, the powers of becoming small, great, light, heavy, attaining what one wills, and the like—are known as the eight siddhis. The thirty-ninth chapter of the Brahmavaivarta Purāna mentions eighteen kinds, but there are many others including such minor accomplishments as nakhadarpaṇa-siddhi or "nailgazing." The great siddhi is spiritual perfection. Even the mighty powers of the "eight siddhis" are known as the "lesser siddhi," since the greatest of all siddhis is full liberation (mahānirvāṇa) from the bonds of phenomenal life and union with the Paramātmā, which is the supreme object (paramārtha) to be attained through human birth.

CPSIA information can be obtained
at www.ICGtesting.com
Printed in the USA
LVHW041956260523
748156LV00001B/129

9 781614 273394